Balthasar Henry Meyer

A History of Early Railroad Legislation in Wisconsin

.

Balthasar Henry Meyer

A History of Early Railroad Legislation in Wisconsin

ISBN/EAN: 9783744724579

Printed in Europe, USA, Canada, Australia, Japan

Cover: Foto ©ninafisch / pixelio.de

More available books at **www.hansebooks.com**

A HISTORY OF EARLY RAILROAD LEGISLATION IN WISCONSIN

BY

BALTHASAR HENRY MEYER, PH. D.

[From Wisconsin Historical Collections, Vol. XIV

MADISON
STATE HISTORICAL SOCIETY OF WISCONSIN
1898

A HISTORY OF EARLY RAILROAD LEGISLATION IN WISCONSIN.[1]

BY BALTHASAR HENRY MEYER, PH. D.

Contents.

CHAPTER I.
Wisconsin railroad history from 1836 to 1851.

CHAPTER II.
Early railroad charters, 1836 to 1853.

APPENDIX.

CHAPTER I.

WISCONSIN RAILROAD HISTORY FROM 1836 TO 1851.

1. *The beginning of the railroad agitation.*

The initial step in the movement which nearly fourteen-and-a-half years later resulted in the opening of the first line

[1] This essay contains the first two chapters of a thesis submitted for the degree of doctor of philosophy, in the University of Wisconsin.

of railroads in Wisconsin, was taken at Milwaukee on Saturday, September 17, 1836. During the evening of that day,
a number of citizens met at one of the hotels to exchange
views and adopt measures in relation to a proposed railroad from Milwaukee to the Mississippi.[1] The local editor
enthusiastically reviewed the meeting, and remarked that
the project had been "favorably noticed abroad."[2] New
York papers, he said, speak of it as of greatest importance
to Wisconsin and to New York. It was one of the favorite
methods of our early editors to appeal to Eastern papers
in support of their projects; although, in many instances,
the quotations or sentiments attributed to New York or
Boston papers were communications written by Western
men. Appearing originally in Eastern papers over the
writer's name, they were, when quoted in Western papers,
frequently attributed simply to the Eastern paper, and not
to the Western inspirer or author. Sometimes, indeed, alleged "indorsements" were often reported in the West,—
such was the case on this occasion,— days before the fast-
est existing mail could have conveyed the news. Be this
as it may, the Milwaukee meeting accomplished its object.
It was decided to petition the Territorial legislature, at its
next session, to pass an act incorporating a company for
the purpose of constructing a railroad from Milwaukee to
the Mississippi, by way of Mineral Point. A committee
of fifteen was appointed to correspond with people of other
parts of the Territory, to circulate petitions, "and in general to take such measures as they may deem proper and
needful to carry into effect the objects of the meeting."
This committee was composed of Samuel Brown, who had
acted as president of the meeting, Byron Kilbourn, its secretary, N. F. Hyer, H. Crocker, Solomon Juneau, William
P. Proudfit, S. D. Hollister, S. W. Dunbar, Horace Chase,
William R. Longstreet, A. B. Morton, James H. Rogers,
B. H. Edgerton, William N. Gardner, and Thomas Holmes.
Such was the beginning of the movement which ultimately

---

[1] Milwaukee *Advertiser*, September 15, 1836.
[2] *Id.*, September 22. There was then no daily paper in Milwaukee.

resulted in what we now know as the Chicago, Milwaukee & St. Paul Railway system.

The same issue of the Milwaukee *Advertiser* which reported the above meeting, contained in its advertising columns an announcement that an application would be made to the Territorial council, at its next session, for an act to incorporate a company to construct a railroad from Milwaukee to the city of Superior. The editor confesses himself so ignorant of the geography of the Territory, and so far behind the age of speculation, that he does not know the location of this northern city; he pertinently protests against chartering a railroad company for the purpose of bringing some town into public notice. Considering the primitive conditions of Wisconsin Territory, such a project was certainly absurd; probably it was designed simply to arouse interest in the Milwaukee & Mississippi Railway. According to the first Territorial census, taken in 1836, Wisconsin's white population probably did not exceed 12,000, nearly all of which was confined to two small areas in the southeastern and the southwestern parts of the Territory,[1] so that one terminus and the whole length of the Milwaukee & Superior R. R. would have lain in an uninhabited country. The journals of the Territorial council and house of representatives for 1836, contain no mention of the Milwaukee & Superior, but record the failure of the Milwaukee & Mississippi scheme. This was due largely to the opposition of the promoters of the Belmont & Dubuque R. R., who secured a charter during this session.[2] At about

[1] Thwaites's "The Territorial Census for 1836," *Wis. Hist. Colls.*, xiii, p. 247, and map. This census was taken in the four counties of Milwaukee, Iowa, Crawford, and Brown, the two latter each including a triangular tract between the St. Croix and Mississippi rivers, and the Menomonee river and Green Bay, respectively (now belonging to Minnesota and to Michigan). These four counties included nearly all of the territory comprised in the present State of Wisconsin, and had a total population of 11,683. The Territory, in 1836, "embraced all of the present Iowa and Minnesota, and the country still farther westward to about the site of Bismarck, N. Dak."

[2] Belmont, Iowa county, was then the capital. Out of a total of seven

the same time the La Fontaine charter, providing for a railroad from La Fontaine, on the Fox River, to Winnebago City, on the northeastern shore of Lake Winnebago,— a distance of about thirteen miles,— was granted. Nothing came of this project.

While the Milwaukee meeting of September, 1836, was the first definite step leading directly towards the organization of the Milwaukee & Mississippi R. R. Co., the agitation dates farther back. On January 13, 1836, Mr. Edgerton, whose name appears in the list of members of the committee given above, and who was at this time a member of the committee on internal improvements of the legislative council of the Territory of Michigan,[1] then in session at Green Bay, reported in favor of a memorial to congress. This calls the attention of congress to the increasing lake traffic, and to the necessity of constructing light-houses and improving harbors. It dwells upon the importance of the Fox, Wisconsin, and Mississippi rivers; and asks for an appropriation to survey them and remove obstructions, asserting that the loss of time, and the damage to vessels and cargo, exceeded ten per cent of the whole amount of merchandise transported — or a dead loss of two hundred thousand dollars annually. It recites delays and injuries of the mails, and difficulties encountered in moving troops from Fort Howard. But the burden of the memorial falls upon the Milwaukee & Mississippi R. R. This railroad, it is asserted, "claims the attention of all who take an interest in the prosperity and growth of our country," and congress is asked to make an appropriation for an examination and survey of the route.

Something may be judged of the importance of this railroad [continue the memorialists], by calculating the immense saving that through its means might be made in transporting lead by way of the Erie Canal to New York. The average cost of transporting this lead to the navigable waters

councillors and fourteen representatives in the legislature, what was then Milwaukee county had two and three members respectively.

[1] Wisconsin was still a part of Michigan Territory. The act establishing Territorial government in Wisconsin was not passed by congress until April 20, 1836.

14

of the Mississippi, is thirty-one cents per hundred pounds. From thence to New York, it is one dollar and twenty-five cents per hundred pounds. By means of a railroad running directly through the heart of the mining country, the cost of transporting this amount to Lake Michigan would but little exceed the present cost of transporting it to the Mississippi. From Lake Michigan, by way of the Erie Canal to New York, the cost of transportation is but forty-two cents per hundred pounds. By allowing the cost of transportation by the way of the railroad to Lake Michigan to be thirty-five cents per hundred pounds, which it will not exceed, the cost of transporting the fourteen million pounds of lead by the different routes would stand thus:

I. By the way of New Orleans.

    31c per 100 for delivering it upon the Mississippi $43,400 00

    $1.25 per 100 from thence to New York.   175,400 00
    _____
    $218,800 00

II. By the way of the Erie Canal.

    35c per 100 to Lake Michigan. $49,000 00

    42c per 100 from thence to New York.   58,800 00
    _____
    $107,800 00

Making a saving in the transportation by way of the Erie Canal, of $110,000 00

Besides this, persons shipping their lead by the way of the Erie canal would be enabled to get the proceeds of their sales at least three months sooner than by the way of New Orleans. Valuing the lead at six cents per pound in New York, and deducting from the sum the amount of the transportation, a balance of seven hundred thirty-two thousand eight hundred dollars is left. The interest upon this amount, at seven per cent for three months lost time, will amount to twelve thousand eight hundred and thirteen dollars, which added to the balance in favor of the Erie canal route will amount to one hundred twenty-three thousand and four hundred thirteen dollars; add to this the saving of imports, and the amount will be nearly doubled.[1]

The weight of the arguments presented in the memorial, clearly group themselves about the lead trade. As late as 1842, at a railroad meeting in Madison, Moses M. Strong stated that the transportation of lead alone would pay six per cent on the investment in the proposed Milwaukee & Mississippi R. R. And this is the way he figured it out: The present output of lead is twenty million pounds annually; shipped by way of New Orleans, it cost $2.50 per hundred; from Lake Michigan to the east, it would cost but 50

_____

[1] Memorial published in Milwaukee *Advertiser*, July 21, 1836.

cents; hence the smelter could well afford to pay 75 cents per hundred to the railroad, saving thereby $1.25, and still give the railroad an annual revenue of $150,000.[1] But how an investment of $2,500,000 could build and equip a railroad from Lake Michigan to the Mississippi, the speaker did not explain; nor did he make it clear that the lead trade could with certainty be so readily deflected from its old southern route.

Even two years later, a Milwaukee editor expressed the belief that the output of lead would soon be so large that its transportation would yield enough to pay a "handsome interest" on such a railroad investment.[2]

The prize of early Wisconsin trade was shot and lead.[3] In the struggle for this prize, there were arrayed against each other St. Louis and New Orleans with their Mississippi and Gulf route on the one hand, and Chicago and New York with their Erie Canal and lake route on the other. This also is brought out in the Green Bay memorial. The agitation for the Milwaukee & Mississippi R. R. was but a part of the larger struggle between the east-and-west route and the north-and-south route. But while the lead trade seems to have been the chief object of this early rivalry, after about 1845 the tendency to overestimate the importance of the lead trade died out, and the agricultural interests gained the ascendency. In 1846, the estimated receipts from tariffs on the traffic between Milwaukee and the Mississippi amounted to $352,000, divided as follows:[4]

Agricultural products	$200,000
Passengers	60,000
Merchandise	50,000
Lead	42,000

It is possible that these figures are not reliable; yet it is fair to assume that they indicate the relative importance

---

[1] *Sentinel and Gazette*, January 29, 1842.

[2] *Id.*, November 20, 1844.

[3] Cf. Libby "The Significance of the Lead and Shot Trade in Early Wisconsin History," *Wis. Hist. Colls.*, vol. xiii, pp. 293ff.

[4] *Sentinel and Gazette*, January 30, 1846.

of the receipts.   Lead, it will be seen, contributed only about twelve per cent of the total.

The growing importance of the wheat trade was re-inforced by the development of the Rock River valley.   In a letter of August 21, 1850, Henry Dodge, writing to R. J. Walker, gives the following figures from the "census taken under Territorial authority:" [1]

	Population in 1840.	1846.
Rock county	1,701	12,405
Jefferson county	904	8,680
Dodge county	67	7,787

These figures clearly indicate an increasing capacity of the Rock River valley to support a railroad.   Beloit and Janesville were henceforth to receive competing bids from Milwaukee, Southport (later Kenosha), Chicago, and the Mississippi towns.   The question was, In what direction shall the surplus produce of this rich valley flow?   The ex-port wheat trade of Milwaukee had risen from 133,310 bushels in 1845 [2] to 2,208,517 bushels in 1849, or a steady annual increase of 100 per cent.; of this, the Rock River valley contributed a large amount.

In 1848, the total imports of Milwaukee amounted to $3,828,650, while the exports were valued at $2,098,469.36, of which 93 per cent was wheat, only $2\frac{1}{2}$ per cent lead and shot, and the remainder hides, pork and beef, and sundries. During the same year, the lead and shot trade of St. Louis had begun its decline.   These facts support the statement made above, concerning the decreasing relative significance of the lead and shot trade after 1845.   Wheat was now the prize.   "Not to speak of mines and lumber, the one, the main and almost the only article of export for Wisconsin, must be wheat." [3]

In the southwestern part of the Territory, sentiment was partly in favor of a railroad to Chicago, due largely to the

---

[1] *Sentinel and Gazette*, September 26, 1850.

[2] *American Railroad Journal*, June 1, 1850, p. 344.

[3] *Id.*, March 6, 1848. See also, *Mineral Point Democrat* of Novem-ber 26, 1845, for statistics which point to the same conclusion.

great influence of Galena, which was pushing the Chicago & Galena R. R. project. Southport (Kenosha) was anxious to build a railroad to Beloit and the south, connecting with the Chicago & Galena. Both these factors, as well as the Rock River Valley R. R. scheme, were obstacles in the way of the Milwaukee & Mississippi. However, on the whole, western Wisconsin ably supported the Milwaukee enterprise. "Oh, for a good road across the territory," are the words with which one editor of that section closes his exhortation. For want of such a road, says another, "the western part of Wisconsin Territory is actually going into decay."[1] Here were farmers, occupying one of the finest agricultural sections of the union, who could dispose of only a small part of their produce, and that altogether for home consumption. The difficulties attendant upon the navigation of the Mississippi, and the consequent high rate of freight, shut them out from a southern outlet, while bad roads to the Lake as effectually prevented them from getting an eastern market. "Large quantities of surplus produce have been left by our farmers to rot upon the ground the past season, for want of a good communication by which to find a market. * * * The positive result of this state of things, if continued, will be the gradual depopulation of the western part of the Territory." At the same time "great numbers" of miners and farmers were migrating to the copper region on Lake Superior, and to Oregon. Such was the "melancholy" condition of western Wisconsin. Perhaps some of these accounts were exaggerated, yet one can not read them without feeling that western Wisconsin was really suffering. Its people were longing for the day when they might share the transportation facilities of their fellows in the eastern part of the state. A tide of emigration was moving westward, with "the spray of the Lake still on their garments," and another was moving eastward from the Mississippi. There was a "suture" between these two waves. Their edges

---

[1] *Grant County Herald*, April 8, 1843.

had not yet united. The river and the lake had been "feeling for each other," and the railroad must unite them, even though "Sin and Death" should get the contract.[1]

The country immediately west of the Mississippi re-echoed these sentiments. Internal-improvement conventions and railroad meetings were held, during various intervals, at McGregor, Dubuque, Keokuk, Cedar Rapids, and other places. A memorial was addressed to the Wisconsin legislature, by the legislature of Iowa, praying for direct communication with the lake. Iowa, a "rich and fast growing State," would then pour her surplus produce into Wisconsin and swell the revenues of this railroad.[2] While the expressions of these meetings and of the legislature may have been inspired largely by men personally interested, they could not have received such wide support had there not been something genuine at the bottom. Economically, southwestern Wisconsin and eastern Iowa were a unit. "Although once united with us,[3] Law and the Mississippi have now divorced the great Territories, Iowa and Wisconsin. If a mountain ridge like the Andes were planted between us, we should not be more effectually separated than we now are because neither Iowa nor Wisconsin would rest until they had bored some holes through Nature's great partition walls, so that they could pass back and forth at less expense than the present cost of ferriage. * * * The position of Iowa, the laws of trade, the boundless resources of Iowa, so rapidly developing, her business and her products swelling and pressing onward to the shores of the Mississippi must and will force a channel of trade eastward through the valleys of the Lakes. Of this business and trade, Dubuque is destined to be the grand depot."[4]

[1] *Grant County Herald*, September 5, 1846.

[2] *Prairie du Chien Patriot*, February 23, 1846; February 28, 1849; January 16, 1850.

[3] It will be remembered that Iowa was at one time a part of Wisconsin Territory.

[4] *Grant County Herald*, October 10, 1846.

This clamor did not fall on deaf ears. Both the Territorial legislatures and governors took up the cry. In his first message (October 26, 1836), Governor Dodge devotes some space to the general question of internal improvements, and then commends the Milwaukee & Mississippi project to the "citizens of Wisconsin who have strong claims on the patronage of the government in granting a donation in land for that important purpose."[1] These alleged claims of Wisconsin to federal patronage were based on the tolls, amounting to "millions of pounds of lead annually," which were paid for the use of the lead mines.[2] The legislature, in response to Governor Dodge's appeal, memorialized congress, setting forth the usual arguments, and asking for an appropriation.[3] Congress finally appropriated $2,000 for a survey.[4] Under the direction of the federal government a topographical engineer actually began the work, but after having examined about twenty miles of the route reported against the plan.[5] Meanwhile five years had elapsed, and at the end of this time the favorite project was sunk in the indifference of a federal engineer. At least, that is the way Wisconsin people looked upon it. They had become comparatively modest, too. I was no longer a railroad to the Rocky Mountains, or even

[1] *House Journal, Wis. Legis.*, 1836, p. 13; Milwaukee *Advertiser*, November 3, 1836.

[2] *Id.*, August 18, 1836.

[3] *Council Journal, Wis. Legis.*, 1836, p. 64. The policy of land grants had been inaugurated by the federal government in 1824; it is therefore not strange that Wisconsin should, so early in her history, have stretched out her hands as others had done. The indifference with which members of congress frequently treated the public domain is wittily reflected in one of the congressional debates on the organization of a Territorial government in Wisconsin. The salary of the governor was under discussion; said one speaker: "It is a matter of perfect indifference whether the salary of the governor is fixed at one cent or at one million. If he is to be superintendent of Indian affairs, and governor of a Territory where there is public land, he will get money enough anyhow." *Annals* 24th cong., 1st sess., p. 3222.

[4] Madison *Enquirer*, December 1, 1838.

[5] Milwaukee *Courier*, August 18, 1841.

to the Mississippi, that Milwaukee was immediately hop-
ing for. If only she could secure one from Milwaukee to
Beloit or Waukesha, that would be better than none. But
ten more years of agitation and scheming were required to
accomplish this result. Not until February 25, 1851, was
the line from Milwaukee to Waukesha opened for traffic.[1]

The necessity of improved means of communication and
transportation during early Wisconsin history, can not be
enlarged upon here. What bad roads are, all of us, unfortunately, may still learn from experience. During the
years of which we have been speaking, it was not a rare
occurrence for an editor to be out of paper, so that subscribers were obliged to content themselves with a half-
sheet or no issue at all. "Out of Paper" was the title of
more than one editorial.[2] The delays in transmitting the
mails were as common in Wisconsin as they had been in
other parts of the country in the same stage of development. Solomon Juneau, postmaster at Milwaukee, found
himself called upon to explain why newspapers and letters
mailed in Milwaukee early in April did not reach Madison
until some time in June.[3] The newspapers contain numerous articles on bad roads, and some of the bad-road experiences are amusing. Thus, the editor of the *Sentinel and
Gazette*, in his account[4] of a trip across Wisconsin, tells us
that in the midst of Rock River woods he "encountered a
man with eight oxen hitched to a half-loaded wagon. The
team seemed rather disproportionate to the load, but the
man gave it as his experience that four yoke of cattle were

[1] *Sentinel and Gazette*, February 25, 1851: "All Aboard for Waukesha.—The cars start for Waukesha at ten o'clock this morning, and
it is particularly desired that all who wish to take part in the excur-
sion be at the depot punctually at the hour named. Dinner will be provided at the Company's Car House at Waukesha, and for those who choose
to remain over night, a Ball offers its attractions in the evening." See
succeeding numbers of the same paper.

[2] *Grant County Herald*, November, 1847; Madison *Enquirer*, November 15, 1839.

[3] *Id.*, July 6, 1839.

[4] October 23, 1848.

not too many to hitch on to a buggy over such roads, and added that for his part he didn't pretend to start out on any kind of business *with anything less than a breaking team!*"

2. *Roads, canals, or railroads?*

Students of railroads in England or Prussia will remember that early railroad projects were opposed not only by people representing the financial interests of canals and highways, but also by those who had not yet been convinced either of their utility or their superiority over existing means of transportation and communication. Postmaster-General van Nageler, of Prussia, scouted the idea of a railroad from Berlin to Potsdam, saying that he was sending a number of mail-coaches daily between these two places, and nobody rode in them. People would better, thought Nageler, throw their money out of the window than invest it in such a nonsensical undertaking as a railroad.   After 1830, Germany was rapidly perfecting her splendid system of chaussées, and these, together with the canals, were thought amply sufficient for her then rapidly-expanding trade.   There was much reason in this.

Or, to take another source of opposition, one remembers the case of the Bavarian *Medicinalkollegium*, who, when asked to give his official opinion on the probable effect of the speed of railway trains — this was shortly before the opening of the first German railroad, Nürnberg-Fürth, in 1833 — on the human system, declared that the rapid motion of trains would cause a derangement of the mind, a sort of *delirium furiosum;* if passengers were foolhardy enough to expose themselves to such a malady it was the duty of the authorities to protect the lookers-on.   Hence this learned physician recommended the building of a high and closely-fitting board fence on both sides of the track.

Aller guten Dinge müssen Drei sein.   Dr. Lardner, an Englishman, made experiments on the Liverpool & Manchester railroad, which led him to conclude that the resistance due to atmospheric pressure increases in a proportion so much greater than the speed, that a velocity of forty miles an hour could not be maintained except at a cost which amounts practically to a prohibition.

In fact, a speed of eight or nine miles was all that it was thought could be generally attained, and a writer in the *Quarterly Review* tells us that a "countryman" of Telford, the great engineer, wrote as follows about a proposed rail-road:

It is certainly some consolation to those who are to be whirled at the rate of eighteen or twenty miles an hour, by means of a high pressure engine, to be told that they are in no danger of being sea-sick while on shore; that they are not to be scalded to death nor drowned by the bursting of the boiler; and that they need not mind being shot by the scattered fragments, or dashed in pieces by flying off, or the breaking of a wheel. But with all these assurances, we should as soon expect the people of Woolwich to suffer themselves to be fired off upon one of Congreve's ricochet rockets, as trust themselves to the mercy of such a machine, going at such a rate. * * * We will back old father Thames against the Woolwich railway for any sum.[1]

Objections like these could find little support in Wisconsin. We had neither roads nor canals; nor had we physicists and physicians who could oppose railroad projects upon such theoretical grounds. Under the spell of politics of great geographical dimensions, which had recently swept over the country, a large element in Wisconsin was ready to plunge into the wildest projects. This will be shown more clearly in a subsequent section. The sad experience of her sisters and neighbors, saved Wisconsin from many of the evils which had befallen them. However, let us first consider the struggle that was carried on between those who preferred roads or canals to railroads, and the grounds upon which this struggle was maintained.

The Fox & Wisconsin rivers improvement agitation, together with the Milwaukee & Rock River canal project, brought the subject of canals before the public and kept it there. The opening of the Fox & Wisconsin route would have been the realization of the highest hopes of Green

---

[1] *Quarterly Review*, xxxi, p. 362. See also *Miners' Free Press* (Mineral Point), June 18, 1839.

1846-50.] WISCONSIN RAILROAD LEGISLATION. 219

Bay.[1] Southwestern Wisconsin was not unwilling to co-
operate with Green Bay to that end. The *Grant County
Herald* of February 6, 1847, in an editorial on "Rivers vs.
Railroads," says that it favors the Portage canal, and that
the Fox & Wisconsin route will secure the Galena and
Potosi lead trade even if there were "forty railroads to Lake
Michigan." The river route would be much cheaper. The
Milwaukee & Mississippi railroad would cost more "than
the entire valuation of personal property in Wisconsin."
In this connection we must remember, as Dr. Libby points
out,[2] that Green Bay citizens owned mines in southwestern
Wisconsin. But northern interests were not then very
strong; and, so far as one may judge by the press, the
southern part of Wisconsin never exhibited much enthusiasm in favor of canals. As early as February 26, 1839, the
editor of the *Milwaukee Sentinel and Gazette* dismisses the
new canal bill with the words: "The Canal Bill will be
found in our columns today. We have neither time nor
room for comment." On December 31, 1846, the Fond du
Lac *Whig* could publish, without protest or comment, a long
letter asserting that the late convention for the Fox &
Wisconsin rivers improvement had done nothing, and that
either a railroad or macadam road was preferable to navigation which it would take years to open. The interests
of Fond du Lac were divided between the Fox & Wisconsin improvement and the Fond du Lac & Sheboygan, and
the Rock River Valley Union railroad projects. After the
middle of the year 1847, railroad interests had gained the
ascendency, although the Fox & Wisconsin scheme retained
considerable importance, as we may judge from a letter
published in the Fond du Lac *Journal* of September 26,
1850, in which Mr. Hobart of Sheboygan, the nominee for
congress, explained his position on the question of internal
improvements, and promised to support the Fox & Wisconsin scheme.[3] How soon railroad interests overshadowed

[1] Fond du Lac *Whig*, December 31, 1846; January 7 and 21, 1847.
[2] Libby's "Significance of the Lead and Shot Trade."
[3] See also Fond du Lac *Whig*, February 18 and March 18, 1847.

the Milwaukee & Rock River Canal project, will be brought
out in the section on the canal lands.

We come now to the struggle between those who advocated certain other kinds of roads and those who favored
railroads.   In this connection, we may consider two sources
of opposition: (1) opposition arising from the belief that
Wisconsin could not yet support railroads, and that macadam or plankroads were more beneficial to the farmers;
(2) opposition due to the alleged monopolistic nature of
railroads.

The Milwaukee *Sentinel and Gazette* of January 6, 1848,
contains the following communication:

Mr. Editor:—I have seen much in your city papers on the subject of
roads; many are advocating Railroads; that is well; but have you capital to
build them, and can you for a great number of years to come, induce foreigners to invest in so new a country as yours? If not, why do you not ad-
vocate Plank Roads? ten miles of which can be built for the cost of one of
Rail Road, and in my opinion they would enhance the value of the farming
interest as well as the general prosperity of your city more than Rail Roads.
Each farmer could take a small interest in the stock, and pay for it in materials for building, and do much of the labor, thus building up your own
prosperity instead of waiting for "dead men's shoes." It is a subject that
the present state of the roads admonishes one should be agitated.

Another letter, published later in the same paper (September 2), asserts that railroad stock will be much below
par after the Milwaukee & Watertown Plank Road has
been built.   The plankroad agitation was at its height in
1848. " Plankroads are the railroads of the people." "Turnpikes and macadams have each had their day. * * * I
would as soon solicit subscriptions for stock in a road to the
moon, than for the building of a turnpike or macadam."
" Plankroad meetings " followed one another in rapid succession in Beaver Dam, Watertown, Fort Atkinson, and
other places.   Long reports of these meetings fill the
newspapers, and letters supporting plankroads are often
found side by side with those advocating railroads.[1]

---

[1] *Sentinel and Gazette*, January 6, 18, 19; February 16, 18, 19, 22,
28, 29; March 21, 28, 31; and April 8, 1848. The *Southport American* (Kenosha), of November 4, 1843, discusses the relative merits of

The fact that farmers could use their own vehicles on plankroads, was a great advantage over railroads, and leads us to the second source of opposition noted above: the monopolistic nature of railroad transportation. One of the objections raised against early railway projects in Prussia

---

canals, macadams, and railroads. It decides, naturally, in favor of railroads, but takes pains to point out why the Southport & Beloit route would be more profitable than the Milwaukee & Mississippi route. Even the editor of the *Sentinel and Gazette*, October 16, 1844, could momentarily so far forget himself as to say: "Our preference * * * would be in favor of a good McAdamized road. On such a road we would drive a borrowed fashionable horse Jehu like." See also *Kenosha Telegraph*, January 17, 1851.

The subject of road-making in Wisconsin is too large to be attempted in this essay. However, in connection with this struggle between roads and railroads, it is interesting to take notice of a book which seems to have exerted considerable influence on the public. I refer to *A Manual of the Principles and Practice of Road-Making, comprising the Location, Construction, and Improvement of Roads, (Common, Macadam, Paved, Planked etc.) and Rail-Roads*, by W. M. Gillespie, A. M., C. E., professor of civil engineering in Union College. This book, an octavo of three hundred and seventy-two pages, had reached its eighth edition in 1855. The Milwaukee *Sentinel and Gazette* of February 19, 1848, has an editorial on it, and it is quoted in occasional letters (*Ibid.*, January 9, 1849) on the subject of roads. How much influence the book really had, I shall not venture to state. However, it seems clear that some of the arguments advanced in favor of plankroads can be traced to this source. Thus, on p. 249 we read: "Plank roads are the *Farmer's Railroads.* He profits most by their construction, though all classes of the community are benefited by such an improvement. * * * The peculiar merit of plank roads is, that the great diminution of friction upon them makes them more akin to railroads than to common roads, with the advantage over railroads, that every one can drive his wagon upon them." Then, after pointing out the possibilities of carrying products to the market at all times and during all seasons, and the consequent rise in the value of contiguous farm lands "to such a degree as to excite the envy and complaints of those living" away from them, he continues: " He [the farmer] can therefore sell cheaper, and yet gain more. The consumer of his produce, wood, etc., gets a better supply of all articles, and at lower prices. The shopkeepers carry on an active trade with their country customers, at times when, were it not for these roads, they would have nothing to do. It is one of those few business arrangements by which all parties gain, and which, therefore, in the words of Clinton, actually 'augment the public wealth.' "

was, that the vehicles used on the chaussée could not be used on railroads, and both Prussian and English law provided for the running of cars by different carriers over the same track.

The following pages will show what the attitude of the public was, as reflected in editorials, letters, and addresses before the railroad problem had become a practical one in Wisconsin.

An editorial in the Milwaukee *Advertiser* of September 15, 1836, contains these words: "* * * nor do we wish to see our Legislature rush headlong into the granting of monopolies, which, however innocent they might be at present, would in the end embarrass Wisconsin in her future Internal Improvement operations, and paralyze the efforts of her people. We wish to see the utility of chartered monopolies, before they receive our sanction."

In our national history this was the period of wild speculation and of financial disaster. Jackson's war on that "most hateful of all monopolies," the United States Bank, had led people in the West to look with suspicion upon the appearance of similar "monsters." It was not strange, therefore, that the people of Wisconsin should have suspected anything which was reputed to be a "monopoly." Thus E. D. Clinton, one of the directors of the Milwaukee & Mississippi railroad, in a letter published in the *Sentinel and Gazette*, June 8, 1849, appeals to the monopoly-hating farmers as follows:

The interests of farmers have always been subject to a ruinous monopoly; which monopoly as used by the capitalists, has always been diametrically opposed to the ultimate success of the farmer. No one will for a moment contend that we have not had to contend with this monopoly; and yet the farmers of the country are those who hold the power to do away with this burden upon their energies. * * * The design of this railroad is ultimately to benefit the farmers of the country, in common with our commercial interests; and how is this to be effected? The farmer owning stock owns also a share in each depot on the line, and the person who has the charge of the depot is *his* agent. Now, supposing, *your* agent in Milwaukee telegraphs to any agent on the line where your wheat is stored, that wheat buyers will give so much for a boat load of wheat; the cars will deposit that wheat in Milwaukee in six hours at the farthest, from the time the order was received. *Thus you will, by taking stock in this railroad, ruin this accursed monopoly,* and at the same time obtain the highest price for your wheat * * * The railroad must be built, and it remains for you to say whether the stock-holders shall consist of enterprising farmers or eastern capitalists. If you refuse to take stock there is no alternative — eastern capital will step in *and we shall forever be cursed with monopolies* * * * Let every farmer who has the interest of the farming community at heart step in ere it is too late.

The *Fond du Lac Journal*[1] laments that the Milwaukee & Fond du Lac railroad bill was "sacrificed upon the altar of bloated monopoly," and speaking of corporations[2] the editor says:

They have always found some way of squandering the funds, despite the checks imposed by legislation; and what has rendered their operations doubly criminal, is the fact that instead of benefiting the public in the least by the advancement of a great work, the funds thus entrusted have been absorbed into the purses of two or three individuals.

Southwestern Wisconsin had had some experiences with "monopolies." By 1843[3] the lead trade seems to have been controlled "by a few wealthy houses" in St. Louis, and there existed a feeling that this combination had succeeded in keeping down the price of lead. Judging by extracts from the *Potosi Republican* given in the *Madison Argus*[4] some agitation was carried on in Grant county at this time. But the *Argus* differs from the opinions of the *Republican.*[5] The former denies that railroads are detrimental to labor, to teaming interests, to tavern-keepers, and to country villages. It holds that corporations are evil only when they are chartered to do that which "ought never to be done by anybody," or that which should never have been made an exclusive privilege, but should have been left open for anybody. But corporations are beneficial when they do

---

[1] March 10, 1853.
[2] February 1, 1850.
[3] *Grant County Herald*, April 8, 1843.
[4] October 12 and November 2, 1847.
[5] It may be mentioned in this connection, that the *Argus* paid much attention to political economy, and published numerous essays (translated) from J. B. Say's works.

that which it is desirable should be done, but which indi-viduals could not, and would never attempt to do. This is the nature of a railway corporation.

In his inaugural address of April 12, 1848,[1] Mayor Byron Kilbourn, of Milwaukee, one of the main spirits in the Milwaukee & Mississippi railroad, expressed himself as follows:

There is in the minds of many an unaccountable misapprehension as to the effect of railroads upon the prosperity of the country through which they pass, and the places at which they terminate. Some look upon them as a monopoly, for the sole benefit of those who build and control them. Others admit that they are beneficial to the country, for the farming in-terests, but injurious to the business towns where they terminate. While others still, claim that they contribute to the wealth of commercial points where they terminate, at the expense of the whole country, and especially to the destruction of inland villages. None of these views are correct. It may be laid down as a general maxim, that whatever facilitates and cheap-ens intercourse among men, in all their pursuits of business, must be to each and to all beneficial. It is beneficial to the producer, especially to the farmer and the miner, for the price of his commodity will be enhanced in value, to the same extent that the cost of transportation is diminished. To the consumer it is beneficial for the commodities which he is compelled to purchase from a foreign market, come to him charged with less expense, as facilities are increased, and transportation reduced. These propositions * * * are so obvious that every reflecting mind will readily embrace them.

In the light of utterances like these, we are confronted with the question, "To what extent did such hopes and fears as to the nature of railroads, find expression in leg-islative enactments?" The answer lies in a subsequent section.

3. *The school fund, and the Milwaukee & Rock River Canal lands.*

In this section we shall briefly consider the attempt made to secure a railroad loan from the school fund, and a re-grant of the canal lands to a railroad company.

In the second constitutional convention, the school fund was the subject of bitter debate. It was stated by Mr.

---

[1] *Sentinel and Gazette*, April 14, 1848.

Lovell that a school fund was not always best for the schools; and the experience of Connecticut and Rhode Island was quoted in support of this statement. Other members, with equal emphasis, denied these assertions. The Madison *Argus*, March 3, 1849, under the head of " Gold, Free Schools, and a Railroad," says that the proceeds from the sales of the school lands will be more than sufficient " to build and put into operation a railroad of the first quality from Lake Michigan to the Mississippi river. * * * In what way can the fund be better expended?" By a plausible array of figures, the editor attempts to show that the traffic of such a road would be sufficient to pay expenses, to keep the railroad in repair and to keep up schools and libraries in addition. Such a road would enable Wisconsin to reap benefits similar to those which New York had gained from the Erie Canal. The constitutionality of the proposed disposition of the school fund could not be drawn into question, because the constitution expressly provides that the fund shall be invested in the "most profitable manner." And what could be more profitable than the Milwaukee & Mississippi railroad? However, should constitutional objections be raised, an amendment granting this power could be adopted.

A railroad convention held in Madison in January, 1850,[1] proposed that the "school fund should be loaned to the company on good security." The editor of the *Sentinel and Gazette* wrote a long editorial favoring the plan, and asserted that the western papers also favored it.[2] There seems to have been good reason for this last assertion, for at a railroad meeting of citizens of Grant county held at Prairie du Chien, the same month, a long series of resolutions was adopted, of which the eighth came out strongly in favor of a loan of the school fund. It is clear that Milwaukee interests were well represented at this meeting. The Madison correspondent of the Prairie du Chien *Patriot* asserted that various "mass meetings" which favored the

---

[1] *Sentinel and Gazette*, January 24, 1850.

[2] *Id.*, January 25, 30; February 6, 26, 1850.

15

application for a loan out of the school fund, had been managed by the railroad people. Their representations were
so fair and plausible that a favorable vote was easily secured. Subsequent developments showed, however, that
the security which could be given was insufficient, and that
consequently the support of the schools would be inade-
quately provided for. "It would be easy," said the company, "to dispose of our stock to foreign capitalists, but
we choose to have the road built by home capital, and
thereby save the profits for home use and consumption,
rather than have them taken off to other states * * * at
the rate * * * of half a million per annum, as is the
case now in Michigan."

The Potosi *Republican* [1] supported the Milwaukee plan:

It has been suggested that the school fund be loaned for this purpose.
* * * The constitution provides that the commissioners shall invest all
moneys arising from the sale of the school lands, as well as all other university and school funds, in such a manner as the legislature may direct.
A safer and more beneficial investment to the interest of the State than
this, could not be made. A lien upon the road itself will be sufficient security to the commissioners, and the profits arising therefrom cannot fail
to more than exceed the interest of the sum loaned, which interest is all
that can be appropriated for the benefit of the schools.

The Potosi editor then recommends the holding of public
meetings in all the counties, to draw up the proper petitions
to the legislature. The editor of the *Patriot* comments:

The suggestion contained in the above article is a good one. The idea
of loaning the school fund of the State for the purpose of constructing a
railroad from the Lake to the Mississippi, was long since entertained, and
we believe first promulgated by a prominent citizen of our village. * * *
The loaning of the school fund for this purpose will obviate the difficulty
(of getting the money). * * * It will afford the best possible investment
of this fund. Its loaning for this purpose will be attended with less trouble
and expense than in any other manner, and therefore the amount yearly
accruing to the use of our schools will be greater than otherwise. Besides
the money will be paid for labor within our own state — the interest will
be sure without any danger of a loss of the capital.

It seems now as if the exhortation of the *Grant County
Herald* of three years before, was to be fulfilled, and that

[1] Quoted in Prairie du Chien *Patriot*, November 28, 1849.

"Sin and Death" were to have the contract, "rather than have no railroad at all."

But while southern Wisconsin was apparently quite ready to enter upon such a raid on the school fund, there were unequivocal signs of a counter-current from the north. Unfortunately the available newspaper material from that section is exceedingly meagre; but there is enough to indicate in which direction sentiment was drifting. The Fond du Lac *Journal* of February 1, 1850, contains the following editorial:

SCHOOL FUND.—That a desperate attempt will be made to swindle the State out of the school fund is getting to be too plain a matter of fact to be questioned; new-fangled projects of loaning it to railroad and other corporations are being daily started, and each scheme, however * * * extravagant it may be, finds its advocates. The Milwaukee & Mississippi R. R. Co. coolly demand of the legislature a loan of only a hundred thousand dollars, preparatory to making a larger haul. * * * The people of northern Wisconsin solemnly protest against the laying of vandal and sacrilegious hands, by the incorporated companies, upon the school fund held sacred and set apart by the laws of the State for the education of present and future generations.

The Sheboygan *Democrat*,[1] discussing the fate of the bill in the legislature, says:

The prompt manner in which they rejected the attempt of the Milwaukee speculators to sink the school fund in a railroad, is a high compliment to their firmness and integrity. Every effort was made and every appliance was brought to bear, to get possession of this sacred fund, and direct it from its legitimate channel. Byron Kilbourn, the projector of a canal that never was made, went up to the capitol with his picked men, made speeches, ate oysters, and drank beer, and as history informs us, they returned with their fine feathers very much in the condition of a peacock's after a rain. We wish our friends of Milwaukee god-speed in every laudable enterprise for the growth and improvement of their town, but when they seek to clog up the fountain of learning and intelligence to increase their wealth and power, we can but congratulate them, and especially their children, in their failure.

The legislative history of this attack on the school fund must next occupy our attention. A memorial of the directors of the railroad, addressed to the senate and assembly, sets forth the importance of the railroad project. It tries

---

[1] Quoted in *Sentinel and Gazette*, February 26, 1850.

to make it clear that "the company presents no features of a monopoly, that it has full confidence in the propriety of such a loan, which would benefit alike the interests of the school fund and of the State,"—for the company could produce "ample data" showing that the "nett income" of the railroad would be above 14 per cent per annum — and, finally, the conditions under which the loan is asked are set forth.[1]

This memorial was referred to a select committee composed of one member each from Walworth, Grant, and Dane counties, and one from the second ward of Milwaukee. There were standing committees on education and school lands, on internal improvements and on roads, bridges, and ferries; and the question naturally arises, Why was the memorial referred to a select committee rather than (say) to the committee on school lands? This select committee submitted a report of some length, and reported a bill authorizing the loan. The committee pointed out the difficulties involved in investing three millions of school money on the plan of district loans and as "the result of its reflections" it urges "the relative insecurity of the fund and its liability to loss, if invested according to the provisions of the present law." Therefore, feeling a "strong solicitude for the complete success in the operation of the school fund," it recommends the investment of that fund in the Milwaukee & Mississippi railroad. The bill was finally defeated by a vote of 41 to 21.

The case of the Milwaukee & Rock River Canal lands throws an interesting side-light on early railroad politics. The lands in question were the 500,000 acres granted by congress to the canal company, and which are now one of the sources of the common school fund. The history of the canal project lies outside of the scope of this essay.[2] While a bare

---

[1] *House Journal, Wis. Legis.*, 1850.

[2] For a history of the Milwaukee & Rock River Canal, consult the last chapter of Strong's *History of Wisconsin Territory;* Lapham's *Milwaukee & Rock River Canal;* and the volume of pamphlets on that subject in the library of the State Historical Society.

beginning was made in building it, for a number of reasons the project was soon recognized as a failure; and an agitation was begun to secure its land-grant for the purpose of building the railroad. Byron Kilbourn was the active agent in securing the canal grant, he was president of the canal company, and later the president of the Milwaukee & Mississippi Railroad Co. In other words, the same men controlled both the canal and the railroad. But the canal was a failure. The railroad must supersede it. Therefore, the directors of the canal company petitioned congress for a re-grant of the canal lands to the directors of the railroad company: "*As a mere Company*, they have no desire for any change; *but as citizens*, the *members* of the company wish to see public interest preserved, which we doubt not it would be in a most effective manner by the construction of a railroad." [1]

When the interests of the Territory of Wisconsin are drawn into consideration, the petition states "that the grant of land was obtained through the *sole* agency of the Canal Company, without any aid or co-operation whatever on the part of the Territory,— so that whatever interest the Territory may have in that grant, has been conferred upon it as a *gratuity* through the *unaided exertions* of the *Canal Company*." Near the close of this same document (p. 33), the petitioner asks: "Is there any better course to pursue, than so to use them as to secure the construction of a rail-road, binding together the great inland seas of our continent with the father of waters, with an iron band; and by means of the business facilities thus secured, binding together indissolubly the people of the remote sections of our favored Territory?"— The "promotion of the interests of all" was inscribed on the banners of all projects, even during Territorial days.

Contemporaneous utterances in the press appear to have been quite unanimously in favor of the desired change in

---

[1] Communication of Byron Kilbourn to the house of representatives, p. 17.

the land grants.   Says the *Sentinel and Gazette*, October 23, 1841:

The Milwaukee & Rock River Canal has been regarded as a project of great importance, and is one which has received the favorable consideration of Congress as well as the public generally. But the mere connection of Lake Michigan with Rock River will not answer the end for which the work was originated, until it shall be continued to the Mississippi; and then the immense expense of such a work renders its construction impracticable, and if constructed, that it should pay the interest upon the money expended. While a Rail Road, besides affording every facility of a canal for purposes of transportation could be built in one quarter of the time, and would be available at all seasons of the year, a canal would be locked up by ice nearly half the time. Another consideration in favor of a Rail Road is the facilities which it would afford for the transportatioh of passengers, the United States mail, the munitions of war to the frontier in cases of difficulty with the Indians. In every point of view a Rail Road would be superior to a canal. And could the grant of land for the Milwaukee & Rock River Canal but be obtained for a Rail Road * * * it would insure a connecting link.

Says the Madison *Argus*, December 5 and 15, 1844:

A canal * * * is a fine affair where it is really needed. But because a canal connecting navigable waters like Lake Erie and the Atlantic ocean has paid for itself, and brought the state a large revenue, it by no means follows that a canal connecting Lake Michigan and Rock River would be equally productive in proportion to cost. A canal is to be made from Milwaukee to the Rock River and there it stops. It connects at the east end with an extensive lake coast, and so far it is very well; but what is there at Rock River? Neither an ocean, nor a lake, nor even a navigable river. There are neither steam-boats nor flat-boats running on Rock River anywhere in the neighborhood of the proposed termination of the canal, and the river will not admit of this kind of navigation to any advantage. * * * The business of the territory naturally extends east and west, and any attempt to turn it north and south into the channels of our shallow river must be an up-stream undertaking.

These were valid objections to the canal project, which must have aided in gathering support for the railroad land-grant scheme. The *Argus*, two years later, when there was more of a railroad fever prevalent, and canal projects had been pushed still farther into the background, gives expression to a feeling of the inadequacy of canals in language more vigorous than elegant. The subject of the editorial is the "Erie Canal," and these are typical expressions:

But, oh ye Yorkers! Do not dream that your old canal, 4 feet by 30, will long be able to perform the labor that is being chalked out for it. Could you see the everlasting west, and imagine the quantities of hog and hominy which it will jam through your canal on its way to the Atlantic coast and so on to the ends of the earth, you would sooner think that it would become as wide and deep as the Hudson, by mere dint of friction. The west! Why, you have not even heard from a quarter of it. And then the Oregon railroad — you need not smile, the thing will be done,— and it will pass through Madison by the way — and the trade with China and all that part of creation (*which is part of the west*) will be crammed into your little, narrow, pent up ditch. It would never do; your whole state would die with the cholic.

In his annual message of December 10, 1841, Governor Doty rather discouraged the Rock River Canal project. He thinks it would have been of greater benefit to have granted the land for a railroad, and recommends the building of "A Rail or McAdamized" road between the Lake and the Mississippi.

The Milwaukee *Courier* [1] contains a series of articles by "Democrat," supporting the position taken by the governor in his message. The issue of February 9, 1842, contains a long extract from an Eastern paper, in which a change in the terms of the canal grant made by congress, is strongly urged; and a postscript to the same letter reads as follows:

Your territory must not think they can get the right kind of men to engage in building a Rail Road for them through so new a country without at least giving the canal lands out and out as a bonus. * * * They must not calculate to eat their bread and butter and keep it too.

4. *Internal improvements in the constitutional conventions. State or private enterprise?*

The struggle over the subject of internal improvements in the constitutional conventions of Wisconsin, was but a reflection of a phase of the larger struggle which had characterized our national history during the preceding decades.

The national system of internal improvements was inaugurated by Jefferson, in 1806, in the Cumberland Road .

---

[1] December 15, 1841; January 12, 1842; and February 2, 1842.

bill. Under the influence of growing nationalism it was
vigorously discussed and temporarily checked in the Bonus
bill of 1816–17. The constitutional phase of the discussion
received a hopeful impulse towards a solution, in the attempt to separate the questions of constitutionality and of
expediency, in the long debates of 1818–19. The failure of
the Cumberland Road bill of 1822, and President Monroe's
scholarly letter, drew into question, with renewed vigor,
the constitutionality of the system. All the old ground
was torn up, and no phase of the question left untouched,
in the protracted debates of 1824. During the administra-
tion of J. Q. Adams, the idea of a system of internal improvements was once more brought prominently before the
public, and in the Maysville Road veto (1830),'it received
its death-blow at the hands of Jackson. This marks the
downfall of a national system of internal improvements.
While the national government still continues to make ap-
propriations, all hopes of establishing a system of internal improvements by direct federal agency,—and from
which the federal government might derive a revenue,—
were abandoned in 1830. Jackson's determination to free
the nation from debt, and to adhere to principles of strict
economy, and his uncompromising hostility to corporate
" monsters," were the forces which dealt the fatal blow.
The new democracy, whose banner Jackson had hoisted,
adopted politics of great geographical dimensions. Expansion was its war-cry. The schemes which were born in
this atmosphere bore on them the stamp of the wide plains
stretching far beyond the dim horizon, and of the great
streams and forests which the new-born "nation" possessed.
The geography of the country had become the main-spring
of the human mind.

The argument, in brief, was this: Internal improvements are a necessity. The federal government cannot undertake them. Therefore, since something must be done,
the States must impose upon themselves this important
duty. The increasing activity of the States in undertaking works of internal improvement, was a characteristic

of the period from 1830 to 1837. The unparalleled success of the Erie Canal was something which every State thought itself capable of repeating in its own projects. We need but recall Jackson's war on the United States Bank, the pet banks, paper money, land bills, the distribution of the surplus, and the specie circulars, in order to bring vividly before us the sequences of the internal improvements and general speculative mania. We are told that the Michigan legislature had "projected one mile of improvement for every 150 of the inhabitants, which, upon common averages, gives one mile for every thirty votes," and that the States had contracted an indebtedness of $200,000,000 "unsecured by any property adequate to the support of such a burden." [1] The atmosphere which had once been the nursery of gigantic projects had now become close and oppressive, not only to citizens of our own country, but to foreigners who had sunk many a fine sovereign in the credit of the States.

The country now entered upon a period of State repudiation, national discredit, and the agitation of federal assumption. [2] The State governments had tried to do what was abandoned by the federal government in 1830, and in the attempt had fallen into disrepute. The pressure for improvements became stronger as the country developed. Their construction had been taken out of the hands of the federal government. The State governments had failed. And now there was but one alternative — not to build them at all, or to leave internal improvements to private corporations. The latter policy was chosen. Jackson's "monster" had now gained the ascendency. The period following 1837 marks the decline of the States as economic agents, and the rise of private corporations. It is into this period that the constitutional conventions of Wisconsin fall, and they must be studied in the light of the events just outlined.

The first constitutional convention met in Madison on

---

[1] H. C. Adams's *Public Debts* (N. Y., 1887), p. 336.

[2] Scott's *Repudiation of State Debts* (N. Y., 1893) gives an excellent account of this phase of our history.

October 5, 1846. Together with other subjects internal improvements was referred to a select committee.[1]   As first introduced, the article was much more restricted in scope, merely stating that internal improvements should forever be encouraged by the government of the State, and providing that the legislature should in no case create or incur a State debt for internal improvements without at the same time providing means for the payment of the interest thereof, and for its final liquidation.   The select committee was then discharged, and the article on improvements, together with that on taxation, was referred to another committee.   Unfortunately neither the journal of the convention, nor the Madison *Argus*, which gives by far the best report of the convention, contains any significant statements made in discussing the article.   A resolution,[2] evidently modeled on the national distribution scheme, was introduced by the member from Sheboygan, but failed to pass.   It reads as follows:

Resolved, That the following be inserted as an article or section in the constitution of this State: That all moneys arising from the sale of public lands which have or may be given to this state for the purpose of internal improvement, except such as are given for a specific purpose, and the five per centum arising from the sale of the public lands, shall be apportioned by the legislature among the several counties in this State in the following manner and no other: One-half thereof shall be distributed among the several counties giving each county an equal sum; the other half to be distributed among the several counties in proportion to the population therein, to be ascertained by the census last taken before such distribution, the moneys to be used by each county for internal improvements therein, in such manner as the inhabitants may direct.

The journal gives no further information.   Articles xii and xiii were finally reported as follows:

ARTICLE XII.   ON INTERNAL IMPROVEMENTS.

Section 1. This State shall encourage internal improvements by individuals, associations, and incorporations, but shall not carry on, or be a party in carrying on, any work of internal improvement, except in cases authorized by the second section of this.

---

[1] *Journal of the Convention.*   See Baker's "Bibliography of the Wisconsin Constitutional Conventions," *Wis. Hist. Soc. Proc.*, 1897.

[2] *Journal*, p. 166.

Section 2. When grants of land or other property shall have been made to the State, specially dedicated by the grant to particular works of internal improvement, the State may carry on such particular works, and shall donate thereto the avails of such grants so dedicated thereto; but shall in no case pledge the faith or credit of the State, or incur any debt or liability for such work of internal improvement.

Section 3. All lands which shall come to the State by forfeiture or escheat, or by grant, where the grant does not specially dedicate the same to any other object shall be held by the State as a part of the State school fund, under the same trusts, reservations, and restrictions as are provided in this constitution in regard to school land proper.

ARTICLE XIII. ON TAXATION, FINANCE AND PUBLIC DEBTS.

Section 3. The credit of the State shall never be given or loaned in aid of any individual, association, or corporation.

To what extent the provisions of article xii contributed to the defeat of the constitution of 1846, is difficult to determine. The press certainly aimed its hostility much more against the articles on banks and banking, and on the rights of married women. However, a letter quoted from the Milwaukee *Courier* and published in the Fond du Lac *Whig* of March 18, 1846, shows that article xii was one of the causes of a division:

"$60,000 LOST!" [The act of congress] donates five per cent of the sale of public lands "for making public roads and canals * * * as the legislature may direct." Now, no *particular* grants are specified in the act, yet the proposed constitution prohibits all such works, except when grants of land or other property shall have been made to the state, especially dedicated by the grant to *particular* works of internal improvements. It is plain that by the act of congress there is no "dedication" of the money to a particular work. If so, what work is it? The Sheboygan & Fond du Lac R. R. Co.? or the Mississippi & Lake Erie Navigation Co.? or the Milwaukee & Rock River Canal? No, manifestly nothing of the kind. And it is equally plain, that unless the act does especially dedicate the money to particular works, should the constitution be adopted, we lose the whole! * * * What say the people to this? * * * Sixty thousand a year LOST, provided the constitution is adopted.

Apparently the editor of the *Whig* approves these sentiments, for in the issue of January 21, 1846, he expresses his dislike for the constitution, on account of the provisions of article xii.

The *Journal and Debates of the Convention* of 1847–48 contains a much better account of this part of the proceedings than the *Journal* of the first convention.   When article xii, on internal improvements, was reported to this convention exactly as it had passed the first convention, Lovell of Racine moved the following amendment to stand as section 3 of article xii:

The five hundred thousand acres of land granted by the United States for purposes of internal improvements, or the avails thereof, shall constitute a perpetual fund, and the interest thereof, together with the five per cent of the nett proceeds of the sales of public lands granted by the United States, for a like purpose shall be Annually appropriated to the construction and repair of roads and bridges in the several counties of the state in proportion to their population, under the direction of the board of supervisors thereof.   Provided that the legislature may at any time by law apply such interest and five per cent to other works of internal improvements; but no such law shall be valid unless it be for some single work or object, and be so submitted to the people at the next general election after its passage, and approved by a majority of the qualified electors voting at such elections.

It will be noticed that this distribution scheme differs in several particulars from that offered to the first convention. First, the basis of distribution is population, whereas in the first it was a compromise between population and area; second, it designates the agent under whose direction the sums distributed shall be expended (the first mentioned no such agent); third, it specifies certain works of internal improvements (the first is general); fourth, it reserves to the State, under certain conditions, the right to engage in works of internal improvements.

Harvey, of Rock county, looked upon this plan with apprehension.   He regarded it as dangerous; the revenues thus accruing would be scattered over so wide a surface, and pass so many diverse agencies in their disbursement, that they would be "wasted and frittered away;" in its practical operations, the plan would place this immense fund where it would be most likely to form a part of a system of political favoritism; the friends of the amendment were fond of calling it the land distribution fund, but they were in fact making it a bribery fund, to be used to favor the interests of party and politicians, and fill the pockets of individuals, without substantial benefits to the people at large.

Another member (Chase, of Fond du Lac) " was confident that two-thirds of the people were opposed to every such proposition," and that we should be burdened with high-salaried disbursing agents to superintend public works.

Another (Root, of Waukesha) objected to the measure because, if there were a fund for the construction of roads, people would "become careless in working them, and rely wholly on that fund."

Byron Kilbourn wanted the fund for the support of pub-lic schools, and advanced the usual arguments in favor of education. Besides, such a system of distribution was in-adequate for undertaking larger works, such as the Mil-waukee & Mississippi railroad, which it would require twenty years to build under this plan. He said also that for thirty years of his life he had seen frittered away in Ohio a fund derived from similar sources and appropriated in a similar way. This speech of Kilbourn marks an in-teresting phase of early railroad politics. In a previous section,[1] we saw under guise of what arguments Kilbourn and his associates sought to secure a change in the grant of the canal lands; we saw how the same men attempted to get a loan of the school fund. It will be noticed that Kilbourn's speech in the convention, in which he favored the retention of the lands and proceeds in the school fund, was made just two years before the legislative raid upon that fund.

Fox, of Dane county, said that he would not make a long speech about the prosperity of New York or the troubles of Michigan because of their internal improvements. If other States had been imprudent or unfortunate in carry-ing out systems of internal improvements, it was no rea-son for prohibiting them among us. Their experience should simply caution us. These improvements were to de-

---

[1] *Ante*, p. 224.

velop the resources of the State, and it was not wise to
put them out of the State's power. The misfortunes of
other States had prejudiced the people against any system
of the kind at the present, and this might be proper; at
all events, it would afford a guarantee that they would not
sanction by their votes any scheme which might be proposed to them, unless it were a proper one. He merely
wished to give the legislature power to submit a law to the
people. It was proper to do this at any time; it was right
to make the improvement whenever the people were in
favor of it, and were willing to tax themselves for that
purpose.

The amendment, standing as section 2 of article xii, was
adopted by a vote of 23 to 14, whereupon Martin, president
of the convention,— this was still in committee of the
whole,— offered another amendment to the effect that when
a donation had been made for any particular improvement,
and was not sufficient for that purpose, the State might
"pledge or appropriate the revenues to be derived from
such work, towards its completion." This was avowedly
based on the experience of Michigan with the Central Railroad. The amendment was likewise adopted by the committee — both of these amendments applied to section 3 of
article xii. Section 2 had likewise been amended and reported back to the convention as follows:

The legislature shall have power at any regular session, to pass a law authorizing a work of internal improvement. Such law shall embrace but
one work or object of improvement, which shall be distinctly specified
therein, and have but two points of termination. And such law shall provide for levying a tax sufficient, with other sources of revenue, to complete
said work within —— years after the passage of the same. And no such
law shall be valid or take effect unless the same shall have been submitted
to a separate and distinct vote of the electors at the next general election
succeeding the passage of said law, and shall have received in its favor a
majority of all the votes cast at such election on that subject.

It was thought that the adoption of this amendment, and
its incorporation in article ·xii of the constitution, would
make it possible for the State to improve the Rock River
and to build the Milwaukee & Mississippi Railroad. The

arguments in opposition deserve a little more attention in detail. It was urged that the attempt to carry out the proposed provision of our constitution would plunge the State " into the gulf of internal improvements " which had swallowed up the credit and prosperity of so many of our sister States. "The State is not the proper person or the proper party to carry on that system;" nor is it a legitimate function of the State government, because of its unequal benefits to the whole people. Again, it was asserted that the State could not carry on such works in as economical a manner as private individuals or corporations; that the actual cost of legislation during the progress of the work, was always a large item in the total costs of such improvements, as in case of the cost of Territorial legislation on the Milwaukee & Rock River Canal, which had far exceeded the amount actually expended on the work; and that as soon as a State government was formed, the State would plunge into such works and become bankrupt like most of the northern States. Besides being a source of expense, such legislation often engendered bitter sectional feelings, as in the case of New York. The provision prohibiting these works by the State, in the last constitution, gave unusual satisfaction to the people, and had often been pointed out as one of the strongest reasons for the adoption of the constitution of 1846. It was feared that a majority, combining the interests of the most populous parts of the State, might impose heavy burdens upon a large minority.

A vote being taken, this section was adopted by a majority of one. An analysis of the vote reveals no striking sectional grouping. Milwaukee was divided in favor, 4 to 3; Rock, which might have been expected to be unanimously in favor, voted in the negative, 4 to 1; the five votes cast by Racine (including Kenosha?) were in the negative, while Grant voted in favor, 4 to 1; Lafayette and Green cast two each in favor; Jefferson, 3 to 1; Waukesha, 2 to 1; Dane, 2 to 1; Walworth, 3 to 2 in favor. Were it not for the vote of Rock county, we might suppose that the prospects of

the Milwaukee & Mississippi Railroad decided the votes of
the counties lying along the route; but it is probable that
the disasters of neighboring States were the controlling
factors. Taking the votes of all the counties lying south of
the northern boundary line of Dane, the result stood 23 to 19
in favor, which clearly indicates that the hope of direct State
aid did not at that time control southern Wisconsin. It is
possible that the personal influence of those who had a
direct interest in the organized canal and railroad companies, had considerable influence in increasing the negative vote. At this point, the journal of the convention
leaves the history of article xii in the dark. The article[1]
was referred to the committee on revision and arrangement,
which reported it for final passage and incorporation into
the constitution as section 10 of article viii, on finance,
as follows:

SECTION X. INTERNAL IMPROVEMENTS.

The State shall never contract any debt for works of internal improvement, or be a party in carrying on such works; but whenever grants of land
or other property shall have been made to the state, especially dedicated
by the grant to particular works of internal improvement, the state may
carry on such particular works, and shall devote the avails of such grants,
and may pledge or appropriate the revenue derived from such works, in
aid of their completion.

Now, by the rules of the convention, every article was to
be referred to the committee on revision and arrangement,
after its third reading and passage (p. 7 of the rules), "who
shall report to the convention all such verbal amendments
as they shall deem expedient, not changing in any manner
the substance of such article." The convention adopted
the article as amended (above) by the decisive vote of 50 to
15; and as adopted, without pointing out many other differences, it reserved to the State the right, under certain con-

---

[1] A member from Racine (Sanders) introduced a very comprehensive
amendment to article xii, embracing nine sections. However, a discussion of it would throw no light on the problem before us. See *Journal*,
p. 351.

ditions, to engage in works of internal improvement.[1] The article as reported from the committee on revision, and as it stands to-day in the constitution, *prohibits* the State from entering upon such works except in case of special grants. At this point the question naturally arises, by what authority and in what manner was such a fundamental change made in article xii? The functions of the committee on revision were restricted to "verbal amendments." A majority vote of the convention could, under the rules, still make any change desirable. But the great change in article xii was apparently made in the committee; and, as reported thereby, the article was adopted by the convention without debate, at least so far as the evidence of the journal goes. It will be remembered that section 2, as amended, was carried by a majority of but one, showing that there was strong opposition to reserving to the State the internal improvement power. In contrast to this vote stands the vote on the passage of the article, 50 to 15. Is it not probable that the opposition voted in favor of the article on its final passage, in order to manipulate it to their own satisfaction in the committee on revision? Let us examine the *personelle* of that committee. In the first place, its members were not appointed until after there had been taken the close vote of 30 to 29, on section 2. It was, however, appointed on the same day, and immediately before the vote was taken on the passage of article xii. As appointed, the committee consisted of Dunn, King, Larrabee, Whiton, and Lovell. On the vote on section 2, Dunn was absent or did not vote; King voted aye, and the other three members no. Dunn had never, in the convention, expressed himself on internal improvements; King had spoken briefly in favor of retaining the right to the State; Larrabee and

---

[1] Following is an analysis of the vote by counties:

	Yea.	No.		Yea.	No.		Yea.	No.
Brown	0	1	Green	1	0	Sheboygan	0	0
Calumet	1	0	Iowa	2	1	Manitowoc.		
Crawford	1	0	Jefferson	3	1	Walworth.	5	0
Chippewa			La Fayette	3	0	Washington	3	0
Columbia.	1	0	Marquette	0	1	Waukesha.	5	1
Dane.	1	2	Winnebago			St. Croix	1	0
Dodge	3(2?)0		Milwaukee	5	2	Portage.	0	1
Fond du Lac	2	0	Racine	5	2			
Grant	1(?)	3(?)	Rock	4	0			

16

Whiton both had spoken against it; and Lovell "believed that the more humble and old-fashioned means of transportation were more generally useful"— in accordance with these views he advocated the distribution scheme favoring "roads and bridges," which we have previously noticed. The committee stood, then, as follows: three opposed State undertakings, one had not committed himself, and one favored it. But in the vote on the passage of article xii, and immediately before it was referred to the committee on revision, all but Lovell voted in favor of the article. Then when these gentlemen reported it back to the convention, they had reversed the fundamental principle of the article, in direct violation of the rules of the convention. It is probable that it escaped the attention of those members of the convention who had opposed its present contents in previous debates, because it was reported as a part of the article on finance, and at the same time with the articles on militia and eminent domain.

Without entering upon a discussion of the controverted question of State or private roads, this presentation would be incomplete without devoting some space to contemporaneous utterances on this question. The Madison *Argus* of December 23, 1845, contains the following in an editorial:

We do not hesitate to express our opinion that a chartered company would be preferable to having it undertaken by Territory or State. We are all aware of the anti-republican tendencies of all chartered associations of wealth, and are opposed to everything of the kind, except in cases where an association of wealth is absolutely essential to the accomplishment of some object of great and obvious public utility. The construction of a railroad is an object of this kind. For a State to construct, control and manage a work of this kind, with profit to itself or advantage to the people, we believe to be entirely out of the question. In matters of economy, governments are always miserable bunglers, and a government railroad would be about as profitable as a government saw-mill.

The same objections do not lie against a railroad charter which may be urged against many other kinds of charters which might be named, because: 1. the aristocratic tendency of associated wealth in the company, is more than counterbalanced by the tendency of the work to secure an equal distribution of wealth throughout the State, and this more than any one principle in social economy tends to keep up and perpetuate republican equality. * * * With a railroad through the Territory, farms in the middle counties would be almost as valuable as any in the Territory, and goods could be afforded in the interior towns nearly or quite as cheap as in Milwaukee. 2. *There is scarcely any chance under a railroad charter, for peculations and frauds upon the public. If they charge exorbitantly for freight, the highway is before us. Travelling fare will be kept within reasonable limits by the competition of stage coaches.* They may run off *from* the track now and then, but they cannot very conveniently run off *with* the track. * * * Still there are prejudices existing in the minds of many in the interior against railroads under any circumstances, arising from an impression that a railroad only benefits the towns at the termini.

The same paper [1] contains an entire column on the constitutional principles of internal improvements. The ground is taken that the time may have been, and may come again, when the State should undertake the building of railroads. Thus, New York rightly built the Erie Canal. But when many states, especially new ones, imitated New York, disaster was the result. At the present time internal improvements should be undertaken by private capitalists, because: 1. Only such routes will be chosen as will prove advantageous to the public. 2. Private capitalists will build at much less expense.

The Potosi *Republican* [2] takes issue with the *Argus*. It holds that the State should undertake internal improvements, paying for them as fast as undertaken, and providing funds by direct taxation. A constitutional amendment should prohibit the State from going into debt for such purposes. Then only such works will be undertaken as the "public exigencies require."

The Fond du Lac *Whig* of January 21, 1847, speaking of the Fox & Wisconsin improvements, says:

We take occasion here to say that in our opinion the work should be in the hands of the state government. The whole state should reap the advantages of the work. * * * We do not like the constitution because it prohibits the making of any work of internal improvement however wise it may be deemed, or however necessary to the welfare of the State.

The Prairie du Chien *Patriot* published a series of essays

---

[1] Issue of October 5, 1847.

[2] Quoted in *Argus*, November 2, 1847.

on the constitution, signed "Old Crawford Forever." The issue of March 2, 1847, contains the following:

ON INTERNAL IMPROVEMENTS.—The provisions of the constitution contrary to the established democratic doctrine on the subject of monopolies, and the great injustice done by it to the new and sparsely settled countries. [1] [The writer thinks it prudent to prohibit the State from pledging its credit, and that] this state shall encourage internal improvements * * * But the great question is what kinds of internal improvements do we need; or are best suited to our circumstances, and how shall this be accomplished? It has been the acknowledged and established doctrine of the dominant party in the Union, since General Jackson made war upon the United States Bank, that monopolies, such as associations and corporations, are dangerous to the true interests of the country, and should therefore, not only not be discouraged, but should be put down. Now, what does the article of the constitution provide for? Why, in plain English, for the greatest monopolies. Internal improvements shall be encouraged by individual associations and corporations. [Illustrated by the Sheboygan & Fond du Lac, Milwaukee & Mississippi, R. R. companies, etc.] The capital stock of these roads must be taken, if taken at all, principally by foreigners. * * * The interest of the public is not consulted nor is it a ruling motive. * * * The interests of the people, therefore, must succumb to the interest of foreign stock-holders. But if the state, when able to do so without contracting debts, should make these roads, they would be under the control of the people, and, of course, be managed for the good of the people. But as it is, the constitution, if adopted, provides for the creation of monopolies with capital stocks of from one-half to two or three millions, and that too in the hands and under the control, principally, of foreigners who would, of course, seek their own interests and not that of the people any further than their own could be promoted by it. (Here the writer figures out the proceeds of the 500,000 acre grant, of the five per cent fund, etc., and advocates the improvement of rivers and the building of common roads rather than railroads.) * * * People of Crawford and the country north, and indeed of all the state, before you vote for the adoption of the Constitution now before us, whether you are a Democrat or a Whig, or anything else, remember that if you vote for it you vote for a system of monopolies of the most dangerous kind; monopolies that will grind you and your produce, who, or which may travel upon their roads, and which by being in existence will prevent the roads from being made. You vote for preventing the making of internal improvements which the state could and ought to make, by directing the funds given expressly for that purpose to another use. * * * You doom the country north to remain a wilderness and do yourselves and others the injustice of cutting off the very means for roads you looked for and expected when you settled the country.

---

[1] This quotation is the *title* of the article.

5. *A proposed system of internal improvements. The Chicago convention.*

The hope of a national system of internal improvements had been abandoned in 1830. The idea, however, still lingered in the minds of the people, and every now and then it was fanned into a revival. The West, especially, had long supported internal improvement schemes, and was even ready to enter upon an alliance with the South, in the hope of receiving the support of that section in securing large land grants. The idea of a system of improvements should be noticed, because in it lie the germs of a tendency towards general railroad legislation. The subject of general legislation ¸will be treated in a subsequent section. Here, we shall consider the attempt to inaugurate a system in Wisconsin.

As early as 1838, there was introduced in the council of the Territory of Wisconsin, "A bill to create and establish a system of internal improvements in the Territory of Wisconsin, on the east side of the Mississippi River."[1] The bill provided (§ 1) for a board of internal improvements consisting of three members, appointed by the governor with the advice of the council, each under (§ 2) one hundred thousand dollar bonds. The board of commissioners (§ 3) shall have power to borrow $1,500,000 in sums not exceeding $300,000 at any one time, on the credit of the State. These loans shall bear not less than 6 per cent interest, and be paid in 30 years. The legislature directs the application of such funds. The proceeds and profits (§ 4) of such improvements are pledged for the payment of principal and interest; and, together with federal land grants and proceeds of land sales, shall form an internal improvement fund. The executive (§ 5) shall issue scrip on such loan certificates whenever requested to do so fly purchasers of such certificates. The remaining three sections of the bill are given up to provisions relating to the board itself.

Newspaper material is extremely scarce for this period.

---

[1] Council file No. 5, in office of secretary of state. I know of no printed copy of this bill.

I have been able to find but one editorial on this bill. The *Miners' Free Press* (Mineral Point) of December 18, 1838, says:

We know of no other way [than that provided for in the above bill] by which to effect these important measures of internal improvements. We must endeavor to get as large an appropriation in land and money from Congress as possible; without which it would be folly for us to enter into the scheme. But before we begin, if we have the means of paying off the debt, when the works shall be completed, without loading the people down with taxes, we shall be able in a few years after to make such other improvements as may be necessary from the revenue derived from those which cost us nothing; we will be a happy and thriving people, enjoying all the advantages of a complete system of internal improvements without having to pay too dearly for the whistle.

Succeeding messages of governors, and the journal of the council, give us no information regarding the consequences of this act, nor do I find later newspaper references to it. So it is probable that it never resulted in more than a temporary agitation.

But a movement which had greater consequences, and which attracted great attention throughout the country, is next to occupy our attention. I refer to the Chicago convention of July, 1847.[1] The circular letter issued by the committee appointed by the citizens of Chicago, sets forth the objects of the meeting at some length. It informs us that public meetings had been held in various sections of the country to consider the high prices of freight and loss of life and property upon Western waters. At all these meetings, "the propriety of holding a convention at some convenient point was discussed and universally concurred in." The fact that Chicago had secured the convention, shows us that Eastern and lake interests had gained the ascendency over Southern and river interests.[2] The high price of freight, and the loss of life and property, were to be the chief subjects of discussion also, of the Chicago con-

---

[1] Wheeler, *Biographical and Political History of Congress*, ii, p. 294; 72 *Niles*, index; *American Railroad Journal*, for 1847; newspapers for 1847, especially from about May to August.

[2] Libby's *Lead and Shot Trade*.

vention. However, the closing paragraph of the circular expressly states that "whatever matters appertain to the prosperity of the West, and to the development of its resources, will come properly" before the convention.

This convention of over 2,500 delegates was non-partisan. There were present whigs and locofocos, governors and congressmen, doctors of divinity and laymen, and newspaper editors from New York and Boston to St. Louis and New Orleans.[1] Representatives of all these classes took part in the discussion. The press "East and West, North and South," had given extended notice of the gathering, and prominent men who could not attend sent letters of regrets. Thus, Henry Clay "should have been happy to assist in the accomplishment" of the objects of the convention; Daniel Webster hopes "the convention may do much good, by enforcing the necessity of exercising these just powers of government;" Thomas H. Benton, like Webster, wrote a long letter dwelling on the importance of internal improvements, but pushes his constitutional objections into the foreground; Van Buren wishes "success to all constitutional efforts;" and Lewis Cass simply regrets that circumstances have put it out of his power to be present. The Milwaukee *Sentinel* and other papers found fault with Cass for his indifference, being himself a Western man. This is only another indication of the prominence the Chicago convention assumed at that time. Silas Wright, D. S. Dickinson, and others also sent letters.

A committee appointed for that purpose, reported a series of fifteen resolutions, declaratory of the sentiments of the convention. They were debated at some length by a number of able speakers and, excepting the last clause of the fifth, unanimously adopted. An executive committee, consisting of two members from each State, was appointed to collect and transmit to congress the proceedings of the convention, and statistical and other matter "calculated to enforce the views of the convention." An analysis of the con-

---

[1] 72 *Niles*, p. 333, gives a list of the editors in attendance.

tents of these resolutions would involve a full discussion of
the subject of internal improvements, both historically and
constitutionally, which, of course, is here out of place. It
is the impulse of the enthusiasm to which this convention
gave rise which bears upon the subject of this essay.

Wisconsin papers, without exception, gave much attention to the convention.[1] The editor of the *Sentinel* says,
"It will be a memorable convention, and the voice uttered
by it * * * will * * * be a voice of power."

It was a grand national[2] convention, and it gave a mighty
impulse to the growing nationalism of that period. At a
public meeting held in Boston[3] for the purpose of electing
delegates to this convention, Josiah Quincy, then mayor of
that city, opened the proceedings with a powerful address
in which the boundless resources and fertility of the West
were enthusiastically depicted. The products of this West
offered great inducements to the people of Boston and
New England to attract trade towards their own harbors.
New York, upon the recommendations of its chamber of
commerce, took similar action. The eyes of the country
were turned toward Chicago and the West. The West
caught the inspiration, and with one triumphant sweep cast
its eyes over the vastness of unsubdued nature and entered
upon a long era of conquest. One cannot read the newspaper accounts of this convention without feeling the buoy-
ancy with which the West rode on the crest of the wave.
"Mr. A. Lincoln of Illinois * * * was called to the stand,"
says one reporter, "and addressed the convention for
tabout en minutes." Thomas Corwin, of Ohio, "the elo-

---

[1] Fond du Lac *Journal*, July 22, 1847; Prairie du Chien *Patriot*, July
15, 1847; Milwaukee *Sentinel*, July 8 to 10, 1847, contain the best accounts, having a full report.

[2] The following states were represented: Connecticut, Florida, Georgia,
Indiana, Illinois, Iowa, Kentucky, Maine, Massachusetts, Michigan, Mis-
souri, New Hampshire, New York, New Jersey, Ohio, Pennsylvania, Rhode
Island, South Carolina, Wisconsin. The total number of delegates is vari-
ously stated at from 2,500 to 5,000. The absence of Louisiana is noticeable.
Was it because New Orleans saw her star overshot by Chicago?

[3] 72 *Niles*, p. 266.

quent wagon boy," appeared on the stage amid the cheers of thousands. Horace Greeley was called for and responded.

How well Wisconsin caught the spirit is shown nowhere so well as in the "sentiments" offered at the annual cele-brations of the Wisconsin Sons of New York.[1] At these an-niversaries, each toast closed with a "sentiment." These sentiments covered a variety of subjects, such as "Wiscon-sin," "Union Now and Forever," "Holland," "Hungary," "New York," "Ireland," "The Pilgrim Fathers," "Our Own Franklin," etc. At the celebration of 1847, the fol-lowing, among many others, were offered:

The Magnetic Telegraph from Milwaukee to Buffalo.— It unites the land of our own birth with the home of our adoption; may it make them one in interest, one in progress, and one in common destiny.

Milwaukee the Banner City of the West.— But twelve years since, a sta-tion for the Indian trader, she now numbers fourteen thousand as her busy population. Having laid her foundations broad and deep in churches and common schools, her course is onward and upward.

New York and Wisconsin.—Jewels worthy of a nation's diadem — the one the acknowledged Empire State of the East; the other destined to be the Empire of the West.

The "age of steam" and similar phrases appear. From the sentiments offered in 1849, we may select the following:

The Milwaukee & Mississippi Railroad.— Projected and (at present) prosecuted by individual energy and enterprise, may it receive the favor-able notice and encouragement of the state legislature, until its Iron Horse shall slake his thirst in the broad Mississippi, and from there may it be adopted by Congress, and extended westward until its iron bands shall en-circle the continent and become the great highway of nations.

Plank Roads.— The small arteries, may they penetrate every avenue of our state.

A Carrier Boy's Address (*Sentinel*) of January 1, 1850, contains the following lines:

> Before I close my annual ditty,
> I fain would sing of our own city;
> Tell of her trade and mammoth blocks,
> Her busy streets and thronging docks,
> And beauty, wit, and enterprise,
> So needful to her onward rise.

---

[1] *Sentinel*, in late December and early January numbers, 1846-49, gives full accounts.

Her Plank Roads smooth as carpet floor,
Bring daily produce to our door;
Soon the Rail-cars with snorting steed,
Shall plough their way through rolling mead,
And lake and river shake the hand,
Across Wisconsin's happy land.

Without multiplying illustrations of this kind, it is clear that Wisconsin had caught the spirit of the great convention; and "felt that something had to be done."

6. *Asa Whitney's Oregon railroad.*[1]

Nothing can more forcibly illustrate what has in a previous section been characterized as politics of great geographical dimensions, than the project of a Pacific railroad. Asa Whitney, its projector, was a New York merchant who had just returned from a trip to China, and his great railroad to the Pacific was to open up the whole Orient. Wisconsin people looked upon China as a part of the West, and the Milwaukee & Mississippi Railroad was to be an important link in the chain that was soon to extend from New York to Oregon and Asia. Even a Fond du Lac editor could hold up before his readers the vision of teas and spices brought to that city over the great railroad "direct from China." As early as 1842, a Milwaukee editor advocated the Milwaukee & Mississippi route because "it would constitute a permanent link in the Great Oregon Railroad, which the indomitable spirit of American enterprise would, at no distant day, exhibit to an admiring world, connecting our Atlantic with our Pacific sea-board." Whitney's journey through Wisconsin (summer of 1845) attracted wide attention, particularly his stay at Prairie du Chien.

---

[1] For particulars of this enterprise, consult: *American Railroad Journal*, 1847, pp. 332, 348; 1849, pp. 519, 631, 645; 1851, pp. 404, 422, 728. 68 *Niles*, pp. 170, 312, 384. *Congressional Globe*, index for 1845–52. Wisconsin references are Milw. *Sentinel and Gazette*, Jan. 29, 1842, May 1, 1848, Jan. 4, 1850; *Grant Co. Herald* (Lancaster), June 28, July 5, 19, Aug. 2, 1845, Dec. 25, 1847, March 3, June 10, 1848; Prairie du Chien *Patriot*, Sept. 22, Dec. 1, 1846, June 15, 1847; Fond du Lac *Whig*, Dec. 31, 1846, Oct. 7, 1847.

A Grant county editor finds delight in the fact that Whitney, in coming West, had not traveled by way of Galena, of which place the editor seemed to have been very jealous; possibly because of the superior advantages which that city would enjoy upon the completion of the Chicago & Galena Railroad.   Soon after Whitney's visit to Prairie du Chien, Ira B. Brunson, a citizen of that place, published letters in which he pointed out the dangers and weaknesses, as he saw them, of Whitney's project.   The latter had asked for a strip of land sixty miles in width, extending from Lake Michigan to the Pacific.   Brunson presented a long array of figures to prove that he could build the Pacific railroad for a grant of land ten miles less in width. Wisconsin railroad politics was closely connected with the Pacific project during the fifteen years between 1840 and 1855.

Whitney's memorial was presented (January 28, 1845) to the house of representatives by a congressman from New York.   It sets forth the great commercial advantages to be derived from the proposed route to the Pacific.   An unbroken line of rails from New York to the ports of western Lake Michigan was about to be completed.   With a trans-continental railroad at its command, the government could concentrate the forces " of our vast country " at any point from Maine to Oregon, "in the short space of eight days."   It would give us direct communication with the Sandwich Islands, Japan, China, Australia, and India.   It would enable the government to send the rapidly-increasing number of immigrants to earn a living on the Western lands, and thus avoid the dangers of vice and crime, into which these classes frequently sink in our Atlantic cities.

In order to accomplish this, the memorialist asks con-gress to set apart a strip of land sixty miles in width, and extending from some part in Wisconsin, between parallels 42 and 45 degrees of north latitude, to the mouth of Columbia River.   Being built at the expense of the public lands, this railroad should be free, except so far as tolls may be levied sufficient to pay the current expenses of operation and repair. A low rate of tolls would accomplish not only this, but it would in addition furnish a handsome surplus for public education. Finally, the memorialist points out that Oregon must soon become a powerful and wealthy State; and, unless united with the East by such a railroad, would establish a separate government, monopolize the valuable fisheries of the Pacific, control the coast trade of Mexico, South America, Japan, China, and the Sandwich Islands, and be our most dangerous and successful rival in the commerce of the world.[1] In a speech which Whitney delivered before the legislature of New York, June 30, 1847, he presented detailed statistics and estimates in support of his project. He dwelt at length upon the expense of time and money involved in voyages to

[1] *Congressional Globe*, 1844–45, p. 218. The same idea is expressed in the Milwaukee *Sentinel* of February 15, 1853: "If we do not soon have a Railroad to the Pacific, we shall have there a rival Republic instead of sister States." Nor were these notions confined to the West. It is probable that, like many other things, these types of argument were imported from the East. A few lines from the New York *Tribune* (editorial March 18, 1850, weekly edition) will illustrate this. The article was written at the time Walker's Pacific Railroad bill was before congress: "* * * but such an attachment can not always be proof against the action of natural causes. California and Oregon can not be expected to remain forever attached to a Government which has its seat at a month's journey from them. The bonds of Empire must become feeble in proportion to the distance over which they are extended. * * * The sure and only sure preventive of this result is a railroad to the Pacific. * * * It would render the political union of this country perpetual. * * * The great result which with certainty must follow the completion of this road is the transfer to it and to the United States of the trade of Asia. The commerce between Europe and the East [Orient] will pass over it. * * * The wealth of every clime will pay its tribute to American labor. * * * A great part of the Asiatic products which will then cross our territory, will be paid for in American products. The vast grain-growing region of the West will then have China for a market. Our corn, which at present on its native soil is comparatively valueless, will then cheaply feed the now starving millions of that populous empire, who will thus become the steady customers of the farmers of the Northern Mississippi Valley. Thus will despotic and pauper Asia be brought into direct and constant relations with republican America.—The world will be enriched, revolutionized, transformed."

numerous ports, and upon the saving which the Pacific
Railroad would make possible.

With great enthusiasm and perseverance, Whitney continued his agitation, addressing societies and business
men's organizations; and in 1851 we find him before the Royal
Geographical Society of London, over which Sir Roderick
Murchison presided, and in the discussions of which Robert
Stephenson took an active part.[1] While Stephenson appeared skeptical about Whitney's presentation, he both
recognized and emphasized the commercial significance
of the project. In our own country, the legislatures of
nineteen or twenty States[2] had endorsed it. It had received the support of the leading chambers of commerce,
particularly that of New York. It had at various times
been reported favorably in congress. It had been supported
warmly in congressional debates. Yet many people felt
that our knowledge of the continent was not adequate to
warrant an undertaking of such magnitude without much
more elaborate surveys than Whitney had made. They
said that his plan did not give sufficient security to the
government, that prominent engineers had not yet pro-
nounced it practicable, and that numerous other objections
prevented them from supporting the plan. This sentiment
was strong enough to defeat the scheme at that time.
However, Whitney continued his agitation, and from about
1852 various members of congress were ready to push "a
railroad to the Pacific." Whitney lived to see the completion
of such an enterprise.

The first east-and-west lines in Wisconsin, especially the
Milwaukee & Mississippi Railroad, were considered a part
of a great trans-continental highway, and thus Whitney's
project gave a powerful impulse to railroad building in this
State.

7. *The element of rivalry. Summary.*

At the present time, talk about a British railroad to
India increases both in volume and earnestness. The Rus-

---

[1] *Railroad Journal*, 1851, p. 422.

[2] *Congressional Globe*, 1848–49, p. 381.

sian railroads across Siberia and China, and through Central
Asia to the Chinese border, appear to have aroused British
jealousy.   An additional stimulus has been given by the new
enterprise to the British India project, which Russia is
pushing post-haste, of a branch from her Central Asian line
through Persia south to the Persian Gulf.[1] The element of
rivalry which in this case is stimulating English sentiment,
manifested itself in numberless ways in Wisconsin railroad
history.   Now it was the competition between companies of
the same city, then again the rivalry between different cities
and villages, or groups of cities and villages; finally, the
local struggle was often but a part of a greater conflict between the commercial interests of different sections of the
country.   In the latter case it usually took the form of a
steady business pressure, while the former phases of rivalry
frequently degenerated into open hostility and bitter personal attacks.[2]   Articles often abounding in abuse and gross
misrepresentations, appear simultaneously in newspapers
in many different localities.   Alleged interviews with well-
known persons were published in New York, Boston, Cin-
cinnati, St. Louis, and other cities, in order to effect or
prevent the sale of certain railroad stock.   Acting upon
public opinion, these wars made and unmade railroad undertakings.

The earliest struggle was that between the Mississippi
route and the Lake & Erie Canal route, which, as we have
already seen, turned in favor of the latter about 1845.[3] Then
there was a struggle between Green Bay, Milwaukee, and
Chicago for the trade of southwestern Wisconsin, which
practically was decided by the decline of the Fox & Wisconsin improvement schemes in favor of the railroad routes

---

[1] "The Week's Current," June 26, 1897, quoted from New York *Tribune*.

[2] Consult Byron Kilbourn's manuscript "History of the Milwaukee &
LaCrosse Land Grant," in the library of the Wisconsin Historical Society.

[3] Henry Fairbank, *Political Economy of Railroads* (London, 1836),
ch. xxi. This author, ten years before the change took place, pointed out
that "commerce [would be] diverted from the western rivers, by railways
to the Atlantic."

to Chicago and Milwaukee. The chartering of the Chicago &
Galena railroad in 1847, and the arrival of its first locomotive
in 1848, was one of the sharpest spurs to arouse Milwaukee
activity.   After Milwaukee had outstripped Sheboygan and
Green Bay in the race for Wisconsin lake supremacy, Racine and Kenosha continued the struggle and prevented
the fixing of an eastern terminus in the charter (1847), just
as Potosi, Cassville, and Prairie du Chien had prevented
the fixing of a western terminus.   Southwestern Wisconsin
held largely with Milwaukee, because of the much-desired
northern route to the Pacific; but when a middle route to
the Pacific seemed probable, that section gave Chicago
greater support.   The editor of the *Grant County Herald*[1]
states one of the problems when he says:

The northern road must be done speedily — done before a central railroad
shall be completed from the Atlantic to St. Louis; for if done now, it becomes the basis of an extension of railroad westward to Oregon; if not done
before the completion of a railroad from the Atlantic to St. Louis, then St.
Louis becomes the starting point of an extension of railroad to the Pacific.
The question is, *shall the upper West or shall the lower West be the
great avenue of trade and commerce*, not only with the heart of this
great continent, but ultimately with the islands of the Pacific, and with
the opulent Indies.[2]

Again, in a stirring editorial, the same writer exclaims
that we must have a railroad. "The northwest is lagging.
The world is running away from us.   Look around us.   See
our undeveloped resources; our fertile lands uncultivated."
He expresses it as his opinion (December 25, 1848) that unless Milwaukee will at once put herself in connection with
western Wisconsin she will be "not exactly a gone sucker,
but her trade will have gone to 'sucker,'" for Chicago

---

[1] December 25, 1847, and June 10, 1848.

[2] That Horace Greeley strongly urged the idea of a great Oriental market,
we have already seen. But one of his arguments in favor of a northern
route to the Pacific, is too novel to be left unnoticed: "The necessity of a
northern rather than a southern route is a natural one. It grows out of
the form of the earth. Everybody knows that the earth is larger around
at the equator than at the poles."— *Weekly Tribune*, editorial, March 18,
1850. In succeeding numbers of the *Tribune*, the Pacific project is argued
vigorously and in detail.

would soon enter her rival's territory. At any rate, he thinks, Milwaukee should at once build to Janesville, and, by connecting with the Chicago & Galena road, give Grant county the advantages of two routes by rail eastward. The editor of the *Sentinel*,[1] commenting on an article in the *Argus*, gives expression to the prevalent spirit of expansion in the following words: "Wisconsin must and will be *the* great thoroughfare from east, to an almost boundless and productive west, beyond the Mississippi." The *Argus*, on its part, referring to the Madison–Janesville–Chicago line, sees no "occasion for rivalry in the construction of these great works."

For about twelve years Wisconsin has been *the* west of the immigrants. This can not continue many years longer, for a vast agricultural *west* stretches away a thousand miles beyond the Mississippi. While our citizens are congratulating themselves that they are finally west, the west is already receding from them, and the state is soon to become emphatically east * * * The living tide, within a few years will pass by us to *western* homes, and their surplus wealth will seek our railroads and water communications, as ours now seeks those farther eastward * * * The question in a few years will be, how can we make the railroad of a capacity to do the business. * * *

Mayor Kilbourn, of Milwaukee, in his inaugural address of April 12, 1848, very clearly set forth the position of the city. No other city on the chain of the northern lakes, said he, possesses higher natural advantages for business than Milwaukee. But these natural advantages may be lost by supineness or indifference on the part of those in whose favor they exist. Art and enterprise may do much to overcome difficulties and disadvantages of position, and change the current of commerce and trade from its natural direction into artificial channels. The history of New York and Boston illustrates this. But just as New York has her Boston, "so Milwaukee has her Chicago, in competition for the rich prize which nature awarded, and designed to be hers." Boston enterprise compelled New York to build her Erie Railroad. Will not Chicago enterprise compel Milwaukee to build the Mississippi Railroad? Unless Milwau-

[1] August 23, 1850.

kee is content to see the business of the finest region of the
country wrested from her grasp, she must do it and without delay.[1]

The editor of the Milwaukee *Courier*[2] dwelt upon the
jealousy existing between New York and Boston:

" They both appreciate the value of western trade.   They are both determined to avail themselves to the greatest possible extent of the advantages to be derived from it; and in order to do this, they are determined, it
would seem, to have a railroad across Wisconsin, if we only give them
leave and do what little we can to aid the work."   Millions of Boston and
New York capital have been idle for years, and " the owners are becoming
impatient for investment.   They have lost all confidence in bank stocks;
state stocks, since the doctrine of repudiation has been started, have become for the most part valueless, and railroad stock has become almost
the only go."

This will be sufficient to show that the element of rivalry
was one of the greatest factors in our early railroad history.
Before passing to the next chapter it may be well, in conclusion, to summarize the chief characteristic of this early
period of agitation.

Our railroad history begins simultaneously with the organization of the Territory in 1836.   Wisconsin was then
but a sparsely-settled frontier region with about 22,000 inhabitants.   In 1840 its population was but 30,945, while by
1850 it had risen to 305,391, and in 1855 to 552,109.   At the
opening of the period, Milwaukee was a village " situated
on both sides of the Milwaukee River about two miles from
its mouth."[3]   It had numerous rivals.   Dubuque, Prairie
du Chien, Mineral Point, and Belmont — which was then
the capital — considered themselves its equals or superiors,
while other lake ports struggled for leadership.   The lead
trade had brought people into the southwestern part, and
with the influx of population into the southeastern part,
there were formed two waves of population moving from

---

[1] See similar expressions in the *Sentinel and Gazette*, February 23,
28, and May 9, 1848.

[2] February 9, 1842.

[3] Milwaukee *Advertiser*, July 14, 1836, contains a description of Milwaukee.

17

opposite sides into the middle region.   The Lake and the
River were "feeling" for each other.   There was an un-
covered "suture" between them.

Manipulating the forces in each of these waves, were the
commercial interests of St. Louis and New Orleans on the
one hand, and New York, Boston, and the lake ports on the
other.   Geographical conditions, together with the relative
decline in commercial importance of the lead trade, resulted
in the ascendency of the east-and-west route; and with this
ascendency, partly as cause and partly as effect, the agitation for a railroad across the Territory increased.   The
project of Whitney, and the expectation of making Wisconsin the emporium of the great West, including China,
Japan, and other Pacific domains, fan this enthusiasm.
Supported by the resolutions of at least eighteen States,
the Pacific road was more than a vision to the people of
Wisconsin.   Iowa sent memorials to our legislature, urging the Milwaukee & Mississippi project, and "once let
the iron horse slake his thirst in the Mississippi, Congress
will send him on to the ocean."   And had not Wisconsin
claims to the patronage of the federal government? Could
this modest demand of the Western child be refused? The
southwestern counties were probably really suffering, and
they were willing to let "Sin and Death have the contract," rather than have no railroad to the lake.

But some of these schemes were too visionary to be taken
seriously.   The Fond du Lac merchant might with some
reason look forward to a time when spices might be delivered at his door "direct from Japan;" but what shall we
say when a bill is introduced into the legislature to incorporate the Port Ulao, Lake Superior, Lake of the Woods,
& Behring Straits Transit Company? Port Ulao was then
a collection of a few huts, and had a pier. To-day, about
twenty miles north of Milwaukee, the traveller may see a
few farm houses, and several piles still holding their heads
above the waves. This is all that is left of a "port" which
could cherish such a gigantic enterprise.

But sentiment was not unanimous.   Jackson's spirit was

abroad. Even in these remote woods, people had heard of a "monster." Some even said that railroads were such monsters. The farmers had been warned against "monopolies." And was there no escape? New York had prospered with her Erie Canal. Then, why not build canals in Wisconsin? Gillespie had declared plankroads to be the "farmers' railroads." Every man could use his own boat on a canal. He could drive, "Jehu like," over a plankroad, with a borrowed horse. There was no monopoly there. He could take his farm wagon and run it over a plankroad or a turnpike, but could he ever use a railroad in that way? His English cousin had invented a wagon which, by a change of wheels, could be used indifferently on railroads, turnpikes, or streets; but the Wisconsin farmer saw no such escape. And would he deliberately subject himself to the dangers of a "monster?" The teamsters, the tavern-keepers, and the village grocers felt that they were threatened with ruin.

We have seen how the promoters of railroad projects attempted to utilize this prevalent hostility to "monopolies," by urging the farmers to subscribe to railroad stock and thus build their own railroad, and have their own agents, their own cars, their own depots, all at their command. That would secure a high price for wheat, and in addition a high rate of profits on their stock. Sentiment was thus not only divided, but it was on both sides grossly distorted. Somehow, the sober after-thought did not assert itself sufficiently; and there were too few men who had well-formulated and correct ideas as to the real nature of railroads, to at once place railway legislation on a rational basis. When once the railroad mania had broken loose, blind enthusiasm reigned, until disaster revived reflection. There is something inspiring in these plans of our fathers for executing great designs with masterful strokes; there is something heroic about the courage displayed; but their lack of reflection casts a shadow over it all. The school fund itself was to be sacrificed. The most specious arguments were advanced to bedaze the unknowing, and the

most despicable means were employed to silence the knowing; while the few who had both courage and insight to
work in the right direction, were lost to sight in the tu-
multuous struggle.

The constitutional conventions met close upon the eve
of disaster in neighboring and Eastern states. These object lessons were brought before the conventions; and, in
harmony with the national drift of the times, the State
was restrained from entering upon works of internal improvements. In view of the legislative methods employed
during the later years of this period, the decision of the
conventions seems to have been a prudent one. The prob-
abilities are that Wisconsin would have repeated not a
little of the experience of Michigan and other states. Yet,
conceding all this, there is nothing to justify the methods
by which the article on internal improvements was incorporated into our constitution. Nevertheless, the question
of State or private railroads was vigorously discussed in
some parts of the State, and it is probable that the majority of the people approved that section of the constitution
when they voted for the whole.

CHAPTER II.

EARLY RAILROAD CHARTERS, 1836 TO 1853.[1]

1. *What the charters contain.* *General provisions.*

A mere glance at the digest in the appendix shows us the heterogeneous character of our early railroad charters. In many of them, not a third of the elements essential to a perfect charter are found; and not five per cent of the charters are even approximately complete. There is hardly a trace of regularity in them. The utter lack of system is the more surprising when we remember that the railroads, for the construction of which these charters were granted, are everywhere essentially alike. Great diversity in law where there exists uniformity of conditions — this is the anomaly presented by our railroad charters.

Each charter names a number of persons who shall act as a board of commissioners, under whose direction may be received subscriptions to the capital stock of the company incorporated by the charter. After notice has been given in certain newspapers, within a specified time, the commissioners may open subscription books, and keep such books open until all the stock has been subscribed; or, may re-open the books, in case all the stock has not been subscribed. Only a few charters require a certain minimum payment at the time of subscription; but all of them require a certain amount to be paid in before the company can organize. The amount which must be subscribed before organization can be effected, bears no fixed ratio to the total amount of the capital stock of the company. After this minimum amount has been subscribed, the commissioners, or a cer-tain number of them, certify under oath that such subscriptions and payments have been made in good faith; and de-

---

[1] See the digest in the appendix.

posit a statement to that effect with the secretary of state (or territory), who thereupon declares the subscribers of such stock and their associates, their successors and assigns, a body corporate and politic by the name and style designated in the charter, with perpetual succession. By that name they have all the privileges and immunities incident to a corporation, thus subordinating each railroad company to the general legislation on the subject of corporations. As such they shall be capable in law of purchasing, holding, selling, leasing, and conveying estate, either real, personal, or mixed, so far as the same may be necessary for the purposes mentioned in the charter. In their corporate name the company may sue and be sued, may have a common seal, which they may alter and renew at pleasure, and generally do all those things which are legally vested in them, for the best interests of the corporation.

After the required amount of stock has been subscribed, the commissioners call a meeting of the stockholders. While the commissioners themselves are required to organize, they can not act in the capacity of the corporation. Only the board of directors can do that. This board is elected by the stockholders, in accordance with the provisions of the charter. Usually members are elected annually, and have the power of filling vacancies in their own ranks. The only qualification uniformly insisted upon is, that a director must be a stockholder. In voting,—excepting the provisions of one charter,—each share has one vote; but no one shall vote on the basis of stock acquired within a certain number of days (usually thirty) immediately preceding such election. Voting by proxy is allowed. The board of directors, in general, has power to manage the affairs of the company. It chooses its own officers and fixes their salaries. It makes by-laws and establishes rules, orders, and regulations; and, usually, the charter provides that these shall not be inconsistent with the constitution of the United States, or of the State or Territory. The board decides the time and proportions in which stockholders shall pay the money due on their respective shares.

Most of the charters limit the amount of the assessment which the board may make at any one time, and provide for a reasonable time in which to make the payment, in default of which such stock uniformly reverts to the company. The board is required to issue certificates of stock to all subscribers, signed by the president, countersigned by the secretary, and sealed with the common seal. One-fourth of the stockholders may call a special meeting on giving notice similar to that required for the regular annual meetings; but no business can be done at these special meetings unless a majority (in value) of the stockholders shall attend in person or by proxy.

The route of the proposed railroad is, as a rule, described only in the most general terms. In some charters, not a single point is fixed. In others, one terminus is loosely mentioned, and the other designated, perhaps, as "some eligible" point on a certain river, in a certain county. The name of the corporation frequently contains the best available description of the projected enterprise. But in one way or another, some mention is made of certain points or localities through which the road is to be built. A number of charters provide for the building of branches; others give the board of directors power to connect their road with other roads; others give the board power to purchase or lease roads; and still others contain all these provisions.

With one exception, each charter grants the company the right of expropriation, and provides for the settling of disputes which may arise in the exercise of this right. It shall be lawful for the officers of the company, their engineers, or agents, to enter upon any lands for the purpose of exploring, surveying, and locating the route of the proposed railroad; and after such route has been fixed, to take possession of the necessary lands. The charters almost uniformly state how much land the company may lawfully take. In case the owners of the land, gravel, stone, or other material cannot come to an agreement with the company, the charters name some authority who shall appoint arbitrators or commissioners, to whom the question is submitted.   In most cases, the charters prescribe norms by which the tribunal appointed for that purpose shall determine the value of the land or material, and the compensation to be paid by the company to the owners.   If such owners are minors, or other persons legally incapacitated, the charter provides for the representation of their interests in these procedures.   An appeal from the decision of the arbitrators or commissioners to certain authorities, and the manner of giving a final decision, is also provided for, as well as the conditions under which the company may use or occupy such lands while the decision is pending.   The company has the right to cross streams and highways; but it shall in no case impede, obstruct, or in any way interfere with these, to such an extent as to inconvenience traffic.   All crossings shall be made in such a manner as to leave the roads in as good a condition as before; and where the railroad divides a farm, the company shall provide at least one passage-way for each farm so divided.

Most of the charters contain some provisions as to rates. The earlier ones are somewhat restrictive, while nearly all the later charters leave the matter of rates entirely in the hands of the company.   Charters which contain a special section on rates or tolls, provide that as soon as the company has constructed a certain number of miles of railroad they may do business and receive tolls; but in charters which contain, among the general powers of the directors, the power to regulate tolls, no such special provision is found.   In the more restrictive charters, annual reports to the legislature are demanded; while most of them simply prescribe that the board of directors shall submit to the stockholders, at their annual meeting, a complete statement of the affairs and proceedings of the company for the year.   A large number of charters contain provisions concerning the liability of stock in payment for debt, and a smaller number have loose statements about the distribution of dividends.   Many of the charters contain a special provision by which the charter is forfeited in case the railroad is not begun within a certain number of years—

and these usually require the road to be finished within a
certain period; while the expenditure of a certain sum
of money in the construction of the road within the
first-time limit, is sometimes provided. Some charters contain all these last provisions, and others only one or two
of them. In the majority of charters, a violation by the
company of any of the provisions of the charter causes
the rights and privileges granted by the same to revert to
the State. Besides, there are penalties provided in case
of injury to the property of the company.

These, in a condensed form, are the general provisions
of the charters of this period. No provisions, not mentioned here, are common to a considerable number of them;
while those provisions, which occur in several, but not in
a sufficient number of charters to warrant their introduc-
tion in the list of general provisions, will be dealt with in
a subsequent section.

2. *Wherein the charters differ.*

In the preceding section we have noticed points of similarity among charters. To point out their differences is a
larger task, because unlikenesses far outnumber likenesses.
Here again an examination of the analytical digest in the
appendix will be helpful.

The number of commissioners varies from one to forty-
one — nine, thirteen, seventeen, and nineteen appearing
most frequently; while a considerable number of charters
provide for an even number. One of the charters names a
single commissioner, who, together with the stockholders,
shall organize — thus omitting the temporary organization of
commissioners, which was the customary preliminary step.
Another charter names three persons who shall act as directors; and a third names eighteen persons who shall at once
form a body corporate. These eighteen have power to choose
a board of nine directors, which power, as we have seen, was
almost invariably delegated to the stockholders. In all
other charters, the formal election by the stockholders of
a board of directors was the significant step, before which

the company had no legal existence; while in this charter, the company comes into existence simultaneously with the granting of the charter.

There is less variation in the number of directors. Nine occurs by far most frequently from 1848 to 1852; while during 1853, thirteen is more common. As a rule these directors choose their own officers; but one charter pro- vides for a president, twelve directors, and such other offi- cers as the stockholders may elect. The later charters fix the number of directors to be elected at the first meeting, but allow changes to be made at any regular meeting, pro- vided the existing board gives proper notice of the change which is contemplated. In these cases the charter pre- scribes both the minimum and maximum numbers,—not less than five nor more than fifteen being most common. A number of the earlier charters secured this same privilege by an amendment. The capital stock varied all the way from $25,000 to $6,000,000, with power to increase to $15,000,000. The power to increase the capital stock is contained only in a few of the later charters. Naturally one would expect the capital stock to have approximately a constant ratio to the number of miles of road to be built; but no such ratio seems to exist. Likewise one would ex- pect a similar ratio between the total stock and the total subscriptions required before an organization can be effected; but this does not seem to be the case. It varies all the way from 2 to 100 per cent. Only in isolated cases is any payment required at the time of making the subscription; but there is great uniformity in the amount required to be actually paid in on each share subscribed, before an organ- ization can be effected. With but one exception, this is $5. This exceptional case requires a payment of only $1, while five charters (out of a total of 59 which fall into this period) mention no such provision. In a few cases the amount of such payments is indicated by naming a certain per cent of the face value of the share.

There is some variety in the provisions about future payments on subscribed stock, with an unmistakable tendency towards less restriction in the charter, to greater power in the board of directors. The charters granted before 1847, and one of those granted in that year, place no restriction on the size of the installments which may be called for, except that thirty days' notice be given. From 1847 to 1852, they contain more definite provisions. They limit the assessments to from 10 to 25 per cent of the face value of the share, and require thirty or sixty days' notice; in two cases, $2.50 on a share of $50; in three, a payment of $12 on shares of $100 was required, while several charters contained no such provisions. One of the charters granted in 1852, and nearly all of those granted in 1853, leave the matter of assessments entirely in the hands of the board of directors; one of them containing the modifying clause that the board should not have power to call for an assessment exceeding $100 for each share (of $100); and still another charter, granted in 1847, levies an additional tax of one per cent per month on all delayed payments of installments.

Incidentally, the size of the shares has already been indicated: namely, $50 and $100. In a few cases only, was the capital stock divided into shares of $50 each. One charter gave each of the first five shares held by the same person one vote, and one vote additional for every five shares in excess of the first five. All other charters gave each share one vote. The period of time during which the company organized under the charter continued to exist, was fixed in only a few of the earlier charters; while the time limits in which the rights and privileges granted had to be exercised, were fixed in the great majority of the charters granted during this period. A common provision required the construction of the railroad to be begun within three years after the granting of the charter; and in several cases there was required during that time an expenditure of from $20,000 to $50,000, in the construction of the road. The time allowed for the completion of the road varied from five to fifteen years — ten years occurring most frequently. Eleven charters contain no such time limits,

while a larger number contain only one time limitation,—
either that in which to begin, or that in which to complete
the construction.   In the case of one charter, these limitations were imposed by an amendment.

A single charter only, outlines definitely the whole route
of the proposed railroad; this is a charter, too, which
in all other respects is the most imperfect of all, and which
provides for the building of a road of minor significance.
Out of about twenty-five provisions which form the basis
of this comparative study, this charter contains but seven.
At the same time it is the only charter which describes
properly the entire route between the termini.   Nearly all
of the charters are remarkable for their lack of definiteness and accuracy in naming termini and in describing the
proposed route.   To what extent this was intentional, and
the means of employing questionable methods, it seems
impossible to determine.   In some instances, subscriptions
to stock were secured under pretense of building the railroad along a certain route; and then a different one was
selected, and additional subscribers sought along the new
route.   For similar purposes, a change of route was secured by an amendment (passed, like all other amendments
to charters, by the legislature).   Lack of harmony in the
legislature, due to rivalry between different localities represented by the members, was another cause of this in-
definiteness.   Thus, in case of the Lake Michigan & Mississippi charter, the Racine faction defeated every attempt
to fix the termini, so that the charter simply says that the
railroad shall be built from "some point on Lake Michigan south of town eight,[1] to a point on the Mississippi
River in Grant county."   In most cases, however, the
termini are definitely named, and frequently a few intermediate points are mentioned.   These are usually embodied
in the charter name of the corporation, which, on the
whole, comprises the description of the route as definitely
as the charter itself.   In many cases, the termini of the

---

[1] Town 8 embraces the northern township of Milwaukee county.

proposed railroad are described as "some eligible point in the town or county of —— to a like point in the town or county of ——," or, "on —— river." In general, the power to determine the route is vested in the board of directors, and this board often has power not only to "locate," but also to "re-locate,"— not only to "construct," but also to "re-construct."

A number of the earliest charters embody no provisions empowering the company to connect its railroad with that of other companies. In order to secure this privilege, the passage of amendments became necessary. Some charters give the company the right to build certain specified branches; but nearly all the charters granted from 1847 forward, give the company the right to extend, connect, or operate its road with that of other companies; those of 1853 usually contain a provision by which the company may lease, operate, or purchase other railroads. Beginning with one charter granted in 1840, and the first two granted in 1852, the charters often contain an express grant of the power of the company to consolidate its capital stock with that of other companies, under a joint board of directors. In a number of charters this power is contained in a separate section; while in others it is given among the general powers of the board of directors; and in still others it is only implied in the power to operate with other railroads, to lease or to purchase them. However, about one-half of the charters of 1852 and 1853 are silent upon this point. One of the charters of 1852 — the same which contains the first mention of consolidation— provides that in case any railroad shall refuse to allow the company incorporated by the charter to connect its road with the same, an appeal may be taken to the supreme court, which may appoint three commissioners under whose direction the dispute shall be settled. No other charters contain this provision.

The subject of expropriation occupies by far the largest amount of space, and only one charter — the first ever granted — does not grant this power. The manner of

settling disputes arising out of the exercise of the power
of expropriation by the company, follows two general
models, that of arbitration and that of an appeal to some
judicial officer, to appoint commissioners. In those cases
in which the charter provided for arbitration, each of the
parties named one arbitrator, and the two thus selected
named a third; the three together, after deciding upon the
necessity of taking the land or material, fixed the amount
of the compensation to be awarded to the owner. In case
the owner was legally incapacitated, the charter provided
for the appointment of an arbitrator to represent the interests of such person or persons. And in case of an appeal, some authority, usually a judge, was named under
whose direction a jury decided upon the case. This
method was provided for in a number of charters up to 1853,
when a slightly modified form of arbitration was employed,
more like the judicial method described below; while in
the preceding years the latter method was most frequently
employed. The later method of arbitration differed from
the earlier, in that it empowered the county judge or the
chairman of the county board of supervisors to appoint
three arbitrators in case the owner or owners refused to
name one.

The method provided for in most of the charters, made
it lawful for the judge of the circuit court of the county
in which the land was situated, on the application of either
party, to appoint three disinterested persons, residing in
the county, whose duty it was to view and examine or survey the land over which the disagreement had arisen, and
to make proper awards of damages. The report of these appraisers or commissioners was made in writing to the circuit judge, and filed with the county clerk of the county.
Thirty days were allowed in which to make an appeal, in
which case a trial by jury was provided for.

A number of earlier charters name the district judge;
one names the "county commissioners;" one names the
county judge or the chairman of the county board of supervisors; a larger number name any judge of the supreme

court; another the chief justice of the supreme court, or
the circuit judge; and still another charter names the circuit judge, "commissioners," county judge, judge of the
supreme court, or the judge of the district court,—notice
the number of *different* authorities in the same charter,—
to perform the functions described in the preceding paragraph as belonging to the circuit judge.   Those charters
which name a judge of the supreme court, allow an appeal
to the circuit court, and the customary jury trial. This "supreme court," however, has probably no reference to the
supreme court of our State constitution. As we shall see
a subsequent section of this chapter, railroad charters in
granted by the legislature of Vermont contain similar provisions; our legislators, when they attempted to adapt
Vermont charters to Wisconsin conditions, forgot that
there were no county officers called supreme judges, in our
State.

The amount of land which a company might acquire,
varied somewhat.   In a few cases the company was allowed
to take possession of as much as "may be necessary;" in
a large number of cases, a strip four or five rods in width
could be taken; in others, 80 or 130 feet; and by the largest
number of charters, the company had the power to
take the necessary land, "not to exceed 100 feet." In several of the earlier charters, ownership of or speculation in
lands, beyond what was actually necessary in the construction of the railroad, was prohibited.   Later charters contain no such prohibition.   In addition to the specified minimum strip of land, it was lawful for the company to take
possession of adjacent lands, when necessary for the purpose of erecting depots ("toll-houses" in most charters),
other buildings and fixtures necessary for the operation of the road, and also to exercise the power of expropriation to secure the necessary gravel, stone, and other
material.   One charter made it lawful for the company to
receive grants of land, and another forbade the company
from cutting through an orchard or garden without the
consent of the owner. This clause was repealed later. A

charter granted in 1852, marks the beginning of land grants by the State legislature. A separate section of this charter grants to the company the usual strip of 100 feet in width, and other lands necessary for construction, wherever the road may pass through lands owned by the State; and it further provides that in case congress should grant any lands for the purpose of building a railroad between the points mentioned in the charter, the company shall receive such a proportion of the congressional grant lying contiguous to finished sections of the road, as the section or sections of the road actually completed bear to the whole length of the surveyed route.[1]

About half of the charters granted before 1853, provide that the appraisers of lands or material shall take into consideration the advantages as well as the disadvantages arising from the building of the railroad; while the juries impanelled to decide on appeals from decisions of appraisers, " shall find the value of the land, or materials so taken or required by said company, and the damages which the owner or owners thereof shall have sustained, or may sustain by the taking of the same, over and above the benefits which will accrue to such owner or owners from the construction of such railroad." About half of the charters granted before 1853, and all those granted during that year, do not mention either advantages or disadvantages in making appraisals. Of the charters which do not contain this provision, a large majority provide for the settling of disputes by arbitration; while most of those which refer disputes directly to some judge, demand a recognition of advantages and disadvantages. In one case, an amendment was secured which empowered the chief justice of the supreme court to appoint (or re-appoint) appraisers annually. Was this to secure the appointment of appraisers from the locality where the road was in process of construction, or was it to favor the company?

---

[1] A late charter embodies the first part of this provision — granting State lands.

Excepting one, the charters of 1848 provide for the completion of at least ten miles of road before the company may open traffic and receive tolls. This provision does not appear at all before 1847, and appears with great irregularity during 1851 and 1852, also in most of the charters of 1853—although in these, only five miles is required. During 1851 and 1852, those requiring five and those requiring ten miles, seem to be about equally divided.

There is some diversity in the provisions on rates in charters granted before 1850. Those of 1850 contain no such provisions, and there is an almost unbroken uniformity in those granted after 1850. This latter uniformity consists in the absence of any and all restrictions on the subject of rates. The first charter granted, reserves to the legislature the power to limit "tolls" at any time. The second fixes the maximum at 6 cents per passenger mile and 15 cents per ton-mile, for goods. The third is like the first. The fourth makes three cents per mile the maximum for passengers, and five cents per ton-mile for freight; but it contains the additional provision that for all transporters using their own conveyances, the maximum toll shall be one-and-a-half cents per ton-mile. The first charters granted in 1847, leave the fixing of rates to the company, but the legislature may alter or reduce the same, provided that such reduction causes the profits of the company not to fall below 12 per cent per annum on the investment. The next charter which was granted, introduced a provision which appears again and again: "On the completion of said rail road, or any portion of the track, not less than ten miles, it shall and may be lawful for the company to demand and receive such sum or sums of money, for passage and freight of persons and property, as they shall from time to time think reasonable." This section appears in all but one of the charters granted in 1853, except that only five miles are called for; while ten out of the fourteen charters granted in 1852, contain no special provision whatever on the subject of rates, and one of those granted during that year seems to be a reversion to type,

18

for it contains nearly all of the restrictive clauses of one of the earliest charters. Nearly all the charters, whether they contain a special provision or not, grant to the board of directors, among numerous other general powers, the power to regulate tolls. This phrase " to regulate tolls," and to establish toll-houses, is persistently retained during the entire period.

The second charter granted in 1853 (Michigan & Wisconsin Transit R. R. Co., to build a railroad from Manitowoc into the northern peninsula of Michigan), is remarkable for a number of its provisions, not the least of which is that on rates: " And said company shall transport merchandise, property, and persons upon said Road without partiality or favor, and with all practicable dispatch, under a penalty for each violation of this provision of one hundred dollars." Here we have the first attempt — conscious or unconscious — of the legislature of Wisconsin to prevent discriminations; this was at a time when the total railroad mileage of the State was 89.27. The transportation of marines, soldiers, sailors, officers of the United States army, ordnance, military stores, munitions of war, United States mail, etc., were excepted from the provisions of this section.

This same charter provides for an annual report to the legislature. The provisions governing this report are much more definite and comprehensive than those of any other charter granted during the period under consideration. On or before a fixed date, the board of directors shall submit to the legislature a report embracing the business of the preceding year, and stating the total length of the road, cost of construction and operation, indebtedness for current work, capital stock actually paid in and subscribed, loans, dividends, receipts from freight and from passenger service, number of through and of way passengers, expenditures for repairs, operation, etc., number of cars and engines, number of men employed, train-miles, etc. The other charters which contain restrictive clauses on rates, either state that the legislature may demand a report at any time, or they fix a date on or before which the board of directors shall submit such a report. The nature and contents of this report, are simply hinted at in the most general way. Charters which contain no restrictive provisions on rates, generally call for a report of the board of directors to the stockholders at the annual meeting, while a considerable number contain no such mandatory provision.

Only one charter expressly makes the individual stockholder liable for the debts of the company, to the amount of the stock held by him. A considerable number of charters declare the stock to be personal property, and then provide, in a separate section, that "the property of every individual invested in the corporation, shall be liable to be taken in execution for the payment of his or her debts, in such manner as is, or may be provided by law; provided, that all debts due the company shall first be paid." This, of course, applies to individual and not to corporate debts. Corporate debts are not specifically provided for in the charters. A little more than a fourth of the charters make the stock subject to execution for private debts, like other personal property; while about three-fourths of them are silent on that point. One of the companies whose charter contained this provision on the liability of stock, later secured an amendment repealing it, so that the stock could no longer be executed for private debts. To what extent the general laws on corporations affected stockholders, will be discussed subsequently.

Not until February 21, 1851, was the charter granted which empowered the company to borrow money. It is quite probable that this provision was incorporated in the charter because of the experience of the Milwaukee & Waukesha (later the Milwaukee & Mississippi, and now the Chicago, Milwaukee & St. Paul) R. R. Co., whose charter granted February 11, 1847, did not grant this power, but who secured an amendment, February 11, 1851, by which that company was authorized to borrow money "for any rate of interest which may be agreed upon by and between

said company, and any person or party of whom such may
be obtained, and make and execute in their name all necessary writings, notes, bonds, or other papers, and make,
execute and deliver such securities in amount and kind as
may be deemed expedient by said corporation, *any law on
the subject of usury in this state or any other state where such
transactions may be made to the contrary notwithstanding.*" This
amendment was incorporated verbatim in the charters
granted during 1851 and 1852, excepting, of course, the
few that were silent on this matter; and several of these
secured a grant of the power to borrow money by amendment. By the beginning of 1853, our legislators had become less imperious, and confined their attention only to
the usury laws of this state,— while in one case, the usury
laws are not mentioned at all. Another charter, like the
rest, grants unlimited power to borrow money, but restricts
the maximum annual rate of interest to 12 per cent.

In a large majority of charters a separate section provides that "this act shall be favorably construed to effect
the purposes thereby intended, and the same is hereby declared to be a public act, and copies thereof printed by
authority of the territory or state, shall be received as
evidence thereof." [1]

With this, we have exhausted the more general features
of the charters. It remains for us to notice those provisions
which occur in only a few, or in but one charter, of this
period. Foremost among these stands a clause prohibiting
banking: "Nothing herein contained shall be construed as
in any way giving to the said company any banking privileges whatever, or any other liberties, privileges or franchises but such as may be necessary or incident to the
making and maintaining of said railroad." This occurs in
a charter granted early in 1847. Not until we reach that
extraordinary charter of 1853, to which reference has re-
peatedly been made, does a similar provision appear. In
the latter, the prohibition is wider in scope: "Nothing

---

[1] Such a provision does not make the charter containing it, a public act.

contained in this act shall extend or be construed to authorize the said company to carry on the business of banking, brokerage, dealing in produce or other business, except what properly belongs to a railroad and transportation company, as in this act provided." The history of the Wisconsin Marine & Fire Insurance Company furnishes an explanation of the incorporation of anti-banking clauses in several railroad charters. Section 2 of the charter of the insurance company, authorized the company to receive deposits and to make loans under certain conditions prescribed in the charter, "or other satisfactory security," and to employ its capital in various ways specified in the charter or "in any other monied transactions or operations for the sole benefit of the company."[1] Although the concluding sentence of this section expressly prohibited banking, the company issued bills in small sums, varying from $1 to $5, under guise of certificates of deposit. The crisis came in 1846, when a bill was introduced in the legislature repealing the charter of the company. This bill involves constitutional and legal questions which, although extremely interesting, can not be discussed here. The opposition to the insurance company was based largely on constitutional grounds, but there were also those who feared that the company would not redeem its bills. The excitement was great, and when Alexander Mitchell, the secretary of the company, sent a communication to the legislature, attempting to explain matters, and offering "to give any further personal security the legislature might see fit to exact in order to secure their issues," a motion to return the communication to him was lost by a majority of but two votes, the house refusing "to show any such small spite."[2] With these extraordinary scenes fresh

---

[1] The charter of the company is found in the *Laws of Wis.*, 1839, p. 64 ff—the last half of section 2 containing the disputed provision. See also newspapers, especially *Sentinel*, from about January 15 to March 1, 1846; Strong's *History of Wisconsin Territory*, p. 491; and *House Journal*, *Wis. Legis.*, 1839, index.

[2] *Sentinel*, January 27, 1846.

in mind, it was not strange that our legislators should have attempted to prohibit the exercise of similar powers by the railroad corporations. But the question at once arises, why was it that only one charter contained such a prohibitory clause, and that a charter representing Milwaukee interests, granted within ten days of the other, should not even mention the subject of banking? The question raised another storm, though less severe, in 1851, when it was alleged that the Rock River Valley Union R. R. Co. had already ordered plates for printing bills, and that certain amendments secured by railroad companies to their charters granted banking privileges.[1] So far as I know, no railroad company ever succeeded in imitating the example of the Wisconsin Marine & Fire Insurance Company.

Seven charters contain provisions for the use of the railroad (track) by different transporters. Five of these authorize any person "using suitable and proper carriages" to use the railroad on payment of the legal toll; and in one case, as was stated above, a maximum rate for such use was prescribed by the charter. The oft-quoted charter of 1853 says that it shall not be lawful for any person to transmit goods or passengers over that road, without the permission or license of the company; while a charter of 1852 provides for the reciprocal use of the railroads, cars, engines, etc., by the road chartered by that act, and all other roads with which it connects. Each is to allow trains of the other to travel over its tracks on terms agreed upon by the officers of the respective companies; and in case of a disagreement as to the terms of such reciprocal use, either party may appeal to the judge of the supreme court, who shall appoint commissioners under whose direction proper terms shall be arranged.[2]

---

[1] *Sentinel*, July 17 and August 21, 1851, editorials and quotations.

[2] We should notice in this connection that these charters provide, not for railroads with locomotives as we know them, but are concerned simply with *rail* roads as distinguished from turnpikes, macadams, or plankroads. What we term a "street car" (tramway) would be a railroad within the meaning of all these charters. They expressely state that the

We have already seen how the charters vary as to the
right of making connections.   One charter authorizes the
supreme court, on the appeal of the company, to appoint
three commissioners who shall arrange the terms on which
that company may connect with any other railroad, in case the
latter should refuse to permit such connection to be made.   A
charter of 1848 permits the company to build the road by
sections.   Several later charters contain the same provision, while others embody it by amendment.   A charter of
1839 reserves to the Territory, or future State, the power
to purchase the road at any time, on payment of the full cost
of construction and equipment, including 7 per cent on the
total outlay.   That same charter contains the provision
that in case of the refusal of any newspaper to publish
certain prescribed notices, such notices shall be given by
" affixing the same to the door of the court house of said
county."   This would indicate a peculiar relation existing
between the contemporary press and these railroad projects.
Beginning with 1848, an occasional charter demands an estimate of the cost of construction of each mile separately.
In several instances, this clause was repealed by subsequent amendments.   A few of the earlier, and most of the
later, charters require the company to build a fence on
both sides of the track, while in a number of cases this
duty is imposed by amendment.   One of the earlier amendments (1850) prohibits the issuing of injunctions except on
ten days' notice.   In isolated cases, claims for wages of
labor, and costs of material, shall be a lien on the property
of the company.   One charter gives claims for unpaid taxes
the first, and individual claims the second lien on corporate property.   And another charter — incorporating a
company to build a road of minor significance — provides
that the personal and real property of the company shall
be taxed in like manner as is individual property.   A

company shall have power " to transport, take and carry property and persons upon the same " (i. e., upon the " single or double track *rail* road "),
" by the power and force of steam, *of animals, or of any mechanical or
other power, or any combination of them.*"

charter of 1851 forbids the company to build the railroad "through any garden, orchard, or building without
having first obtained the consent" of the owner. That
is, if the owner objected to the railroad, he could force
the company to build *around* his "garden, orchard, or
building." Two years later, this clause was repealed by
amendment. Only in isolated instances do the charters speak
of depots, station-houses, etc.,—toll-houses, tolls, toll-regu-
lations, being the words used instead. Having now seen
what the charters contain and wherein they differ, we shall
next notice what they do *not* contain.

3. *What the charters do not contain.*

A full discussion of the problems involved in this section, would lead us into a detailed analysis of our entire
railroad history; no such attempt will be made. The railroad industry presents features peculiarly its own, and all
that will be attempted here is to point out, in a general
way, in what respects the charters do not meet the peculiar
demands of that industry. At the time when railroad
building was begun in Wisconsin, the subject had been before the public for twenty years, and the results of the experience of other countries, as well as of the older sections
of our own country, were available to our legislators. Par-
liamentary debates and statesmanlike discussions on railroads, covering every phase of the entire field as it then
existed, had been published in every great country of
Europe. This section will indicate to what extent the legislators of Wisconsin did not avail themselves of this information, just as the previous sections have told us to what
extent they did embody in their own legislation the provisions of the best legislation of other States.

In the first place, it would seem self-evident that the
proposed railroads should serve public interests, and that
objective proof should be offered to show that this would
be the case. Reliable information as to the movement of
persons and goods between the places and along the route
of the projected roads, would be necessary for a proper

conception of the purely business point-of-view of the undertaking. Accurate technical information would be indispensable for even approximate estimates of costs, and for an intelligent decision on the practicability of the project. On these matters, the charters are silent. But not only must the financial interests of the company immediately involved be considered; the railroad already constructed or projected should weigh heavily in deliberations over new charters. A railroad powerfully affects existing conditions, and the good and evil effects of a new line should be carefully formulated. Prosperous existing roads may be crippled, and other sound industrial conditions severely shaken, by the indiscriminate granting of charters for new roads. The possible effect on all existing economic interests should be a powerful factor in deciding on the merits of new projects. I have been unable to find a record of even superficial deliberation along these lines, beyond isolated conjectures of frenzied enthusiasts and glib phrases of selfish designers. Now and then there is an echo of a voice of warning, but the charters contain not even a suggestion of the results of deliberation.

There are no great mountains in Wisconsin, nor have we extended morasses and wastes. The technical difficulties of railroading in Wisconsin are not serious. Yet, such as they are, every route has its technical problems, and no estimate of costs can be taken seriously unless these have been carefully determined for every rod of the way. And how can the amount of the capital stock authorized by the charter be anything but a mere guess, so long as our legislators have absolutely no means of knowing the expense involved in executing the project for which they fix the amount of stock in the charter?

We have seen that in a few charters an estimate of costs for each separate mile was called for, and that in one instance this provision was repealed. But granted that every charter had embodied the same provision, what would have been gained? Who was legally responsible for such an estimate? Just what should such an estimate include?

To whom should the report be sent, and what authority had power to accept or reject it? Who was to coerce the projectors into doing their duty in this respect, and who could legally interpose and prevent the execution of the project in case the estimates had not been properly made? We need but suggest these questions, in order to expose the utter inadequacy of charter provisions.

A few charters demanded a small payment on stock at the time of subscription. The great majority of them provided for a similar payment before the company could organize and enter into existence as a legal body. Who was there to enforce these provisions? Who could give assurance that every subscriber paid what was required of others,—especially when we find a certain group of men acting as commissioners in half a dozen or more projects involving a total outlay, in their execution, of many millions? And what security was ever given (or asked) by the incorporators, for the faithful performance of charter duties? And in case the road was ever built, upon whom could stockholders, not actively engaged in the construction, call for a reliable statement of the condition of the road when it was opened for traffic?

In a time when every other project "guarantees" 15 per cent annually, some provision should be made for the future. Prudent business management accumulates a reserve for reverses. Accidents may cause losses, and the elements may ruin tracks and equipments. Even without business reverses and destructive floods and storms, the rolling stock will wear out, and the superstructure as well as the road-bed need repairs. Without proper foresight, an unfortunate coincidence of several of these negative forces may embarrass or even disable a railroad. Then there is capital stock, and the bonds, which should gradually be paid off. Yet not a single charter provides for the accumulation of a renewal, building, reserve, amortization or sinking fund.

The subject of expropriation is, perhaps, more than any other, extensively considered in the charters. In another place, we shall see in what manner the right was executed. The charters require the railroad company to put highways which they cross, in as good a condition as they had been before. Who had authority to decide on the condition of these highways, or what tribunal was authorized to hear complaints? A considerable number of charters do not reserve to the legislature the right to annul them in case of a violation of their provisions. And was it not argued, as in case of the Marine & Fire Insurance Company, that a charter containing no such reservation was a contract, and could not be repealed by the legislature? Then, what remedy was there for even the grossest violation of charter privileges?

Most of the charters authorize connections with other roads; but only a single charter names an authority which may force another railroad to permit a junction with a road desiring such connection. Was it possible, under these conditions, ever to operate the railroads as a system? Is not the idea of a system fundamental in every rational ordering of railway transportation?

We have seen, in the preceding section, what charter provisions were enacted on the subject of rates. To discuss what was not provided for, would involve everything that should have been provided for. The matter of railroad crossings, safety appliances, and other precautionary measures, regularity and uniformity of reports, and various other phases of railroading which have been so prominent for many years in the past, will not be discussed here. Enough has been given to illustrate the relation of legislative enactments to railroads, as they existed at that time, and to show that our early legislators did not greatly exert themselves in order to profit by the experience of others. They themselves might have encountered difficulties in attempting to explain why two charters, granted the same day, should have embodied such different, and often diverse, principles; or, why a company incorporated on Monday should have been entrusted with latitudinous powers, while a similar act on Saturday should have placed restrictions on that same power, although it was to be exercised under identical conditions.

4. *Sources of the charters. Summary.*

Were we to take one charter granted by Massachusetts, another by New York, by Pennsylvania, Maryland, South Carolina, Michigan, and Illinois, and cut all these up in such a way that each clipping should contain one charter provision; were we to put clippings containing like provisions into the same box, shake them up, and then, blindfolded, pick out one clipping from each box, the clipping thus held in the hand could easily be arranged in such a way as to compose a railroad charter which in all essentials would be similar to those granted during that period by the legislature of Wisconsin. Even though half-a-dozen or a dozen boxes had not been touched, the resulting charter might still be made quite as complete as a number of Wisconsin charters.

Were I to name the charters of any one State which served as a model for Wisconsin charters, I should specify Pennsylvania, although New York comes almost as near. One Wisconsin charter[1] is clearly modeled on the charter of the Pennsylvania railroad; or rather, I should say that it is a mutilated edition of that charter. Like most of the Wisconsin charters, the Pennsylvania and Maryland charters name a number of persons who act as commissioners, under whose direction a " body politic " is organized; while the charters of New York name, in the first section, a number of persons who are declared to be "a body politic," and in a subsequent section the commissioners are named. Vermont charters declare future stockholders a " body corporate." Both New York and Vermont forms appear in Wisconsin charters, but the Pennsylvania and Maryland form is much more general. In Illinois, both the New York and Pennsylvania forms appear, while the legislature of Indiana formed a precedent for Wisconsin in granting to her railroads the right of way through State (swamp) lands.

---

[1] Fond du Lac & Sheboygan.

The provision prohibiting banking, brokerage, dealing in produce, etc., had its counterpart in earlier Michigan and Illinois charters. We have seen that a large number of Wisconsin charters made it obligatory for appraisers to consider both the advantages and disadvantages accruing to owners. Similar provisions are found in the charters of Pennsylvania, Maryland, South Carolina, and some of those of Massachusetts, but not in those of New York.

The words "toll," "to regulate toll," occur in all the charters of other states which I have examined, as does the expression "to transport and carry property and persons upon the same, by the power and force of steam or animals, or of any mechanical power, or of any combination of such power and force," or equivalent expressions.[1] As we shall see later, the history of Wisconsin charters, like the history of the charters of her sister States, begins with the English canal legislation of the middle of the seventeenth century. But as early as 1840[2] English law restricted the use of the word railway so as to exclude tramways. "The word railway * * * shall be construed to extend to all railways constructed under the powers of any Act of Parliament, and intended for the conveyance of passengers in or upon carriages drawn or impelled by the power of steam or by any other mechanical power." Wisconsin charters follow the precedent set by the charters of at least a dozen States, in prescribing regulations for the use of the railroad by different transporters and in giving to the company the power to determine what kinds of carriages shall be used. This also is a contribution of English law, similar provisions having been embodied in the Liverpool & Manchester charter, and even in the Railways Clauses Act of 1845: "And upon payment of the tolls from time to time demandable all companies and persons shall be entitled to use the railway with engines and carriages prop-

---

[1] This, however, was more than fiction, for the earliest American railroads were operated by horses, mules, stationary engines, or by mere force of gravity.

[2] Railway Regulation Act, 1840, § 21.

erly constructed "—? 92; "No carriage shall pass along or
be upon the railway * * * unless such carriage be at
all times, so long as it shall be used or shall remain on the
railway, of the construction and in the condition which the
regulations of the company for the time being shall require "— ? 117.[1] An early English work [2] contains a description of carriages "which are intended to be transferred
from the Rail-way wheels to others capable of travelling on
streets." In passing, we may notice that one of the strong
arguments advanced in Germany against railroads was,
that the railway coaches could not be used on the *chaussée*
or vice versa.

Allowing each share one vote, seems to have been the
general custom, although the one exception we have noticed in Wisconsin charters finds its counterpart in charters of South Carolina, which outline a system of voting
according to the formula: Any person holding not less
than x nor more than y shares, shall be entitled to z votes.
Wisconsin charter clauses fixing maximum rates find their
counterpart in charters of Maine, Pennsylvania, and Massachusetts; those of Maine being worded more nearly like
those of Wisconsin, than the others. In many of the
charters of other States, I find legislative reservations
authorizing the State to purchase the road, and to change
or to alter rates. In New Hampshire, where general legislation was early enacted, a charter was granted [3] which reserved to the legislature the right to repeal the same
"whenever in the opinion of the legislature the public
good shall require it." Some Massachusetts charters for-
bid the building of competitive lines within a certain time.
Provisions covering expropriation are similar in the different States. Vermont charters provide for the appointment of appraisers by any two judges of the supreme
court. But these supreme judges were county officers, and

[1] Railways Clauses Act, of 1845.

[2] Wood's *Practical Treatise on Railroads* (Amer. ed., Phila., 1832),
chap. iii.

[3] Laws of N. H., 1841, p. 582.

it seems probable, as we have already noticed (p. 271), that Wisconsin charters embodied like provisions without taking notice of the difference between the supreme court in Wisconsin and the court of that name in Vermont. Maine charters mention county commissioners; when Wisconsin charters designate the same officers, it is probable that similar differences were not noticed. At any rate, when, as is the case in several Wisconsin charters, a number of different authorities are named, any one of whom may perform the same function, it looks as though charter provisions of several other States had been consolidated to form a very loose provision in a Wisconsin charter; else, how could a charter assign duties to "county commissioners," when neither the constitution of Wisconsin nor the statutes provide for such officers. The great majority of Wisconsin charters are more definite; these exceptional cases, however, serve to illustrate legislative methods. Calling upon any justice of the peace to issue a warrant for the sheriff to summon a jury for the purpose of making appraisals, seems to have been a very general provision of charters of other States. This is the method adopted by the earliest Wisconsin charters; while almost all the later charters call upon the circuit judge to appoint appraisers.

It would be a tedious task to follow out this comparison in all its details. The "forms" of New York and Pennsylvania charters have been spoken of; but, after all, such "forms" exist only in a limited sense. On the whole, the charters of these States are much alike, and Wisconsin charters differ from those of either, largely in the omission of restrictive clauses, and in having been drawn up with apparent lack of care. Charters of States like Massachusetts and Maryland, show greater care in their construction, and are more restrictive. But the similarity existing among the charters of all the States, which I have examined, is so great as to indicate at a glance their common origin. They may have become mutilated and more loosely constructed in their march westward, but they never lose the character of their English prototypes. It is toward these, that we will now turn our attention.

In order, in brief space, to indicate properly the connection between our own and the English charters, a series of parallel readings is here introduced.   The first column contains extracts from the charter of the Liverpool & Manchester Rail Road, granted by parliament on May 5, 1826; and the second contains corresponding parts of Wisconsin railroad charters, the numbers in parentheses indicating the corresponding number of the charter, in the appended digest, from which the extract is taken:

1. Whereas the making and maintaining of a Railway * * * from or near the town of Liverpool * * * to the town of Manchester * * * will be of great Advantage to the Inhabitants of the said County, Towns, and Places * * * ; and * * * will be of great public Utility * * *   And whereas the several Persons herein-after named are willing and desirous, at their own Costs and Charges, to make and maintain such a Railway or Tramroad and Branches; but the same can not be effected without the Aid and Authority of Parliament: May it therefore please Your Majesty that it may be enacted * * *

1. Whereas, it hath been represented by ——, in his memorial to the legislature, that a railroad from Philadelphia to Columbia would greatly facilitate the transport between those two places, suggesting also that he hath made important improvements in the construction of rail ways; and praying that in order to carry such beneficial purposes into effect himself and his associates may be * * *   [Acts of the General Assembly of Penn., 1822-23, chap. 5407, passed March 31, 1823. Book no. xix, p. 353.]

2. That the Most Noble George Granville Marquess of ——,——,——, * * * and all and every other Person or Persons, Body and Bodies Politic and Corporate, who shall hereafter become Subscribers to the said Undertaking, and their several and respective Successors, Executors, Administrators, and Assigns, shall be and hereby are united into a Company for making, completing, and maintaining the said Railway * * * and for that Purpose shall

2. That James M. Kane,——, * * * together with * * * such other persons, as may hereafter become associated with them in the manner hereafter prescribed, their successors and assigns, be and they are hereby created a body corporate, by the name of the " Pekatonica and Mississippi Rail Road Company," and by that name shall be, and are hereby made capable in law to purchase, hold and enjoy and retain to them and their successors, lands,

be one Body Corporate, by the Name and Style of "The Liverpool and Manchester Railway Company," and by that Name shall and may sue and be sued; and the said Company shall have Power and Authority, from and after the passing of this Act, and at all Times thereafter, to purchase and hold Lands and Hereditaments to them and their Successors and Assigns, for the Use of the said Undertaking and Works, and also to sell and dispose of the said Lands and Hereditaments again, in manner by this act Directed, without incurring any of the Penalties or Forfeitures of the Statute of Mortmain.

3. That for the Purposes of this Act the said Company, their Deputies, Servants, Agents, Surveyors, and Workmen, shall be and they are hereby authorized and empowered to enter into and upon the Lands and Grounds of any Body Politic, Corporate, or Collegiate whatsoever, according to the Provisions and Directions of this Act, and to survey and take Levels of the same or any Part thereof;

4. That the Lands and Grounds to be taken or used for the Purposes of this Act shall not exceed Twenty-two Yards in Breadth, except * * *

5. Said Verdicts and Judgments * * * shall be kept by the Clerk of the Peace for the County in which the matter of Dispute shall have arisen, among the records of the Quarter Sessions for such County, and shall be deemed Records * * *

6. That in every Case where the Verdict * * * shall be given for

tenements, and hereditaments so far as may be necessary for the purpose of said rail road, and the same to sell, grant, rent or in any manner dispose of, to contract and be contracted with, sue and be sued, implead and be impleaded, answer and be answered, defend and be defended, and also to make, have and use a common seal, and the same to alter, break or renew at their pleasure * * * (4)

3. It shall be lawful for said company, their officers, engineers, and agents, to enter upon any land for the purpose of exploring, surveying, and locating the route of said railroad, doing thereto no unnecessary damage * * * (28)

4. It shall be lawful for them * * * to enter upon, take possession of, and use such lands, to the width of four rods (except * * *). (7)

5. And shall return the same * * * to the clerk of the circuit court of the county in which they reside, and it shall be the duty of the said clerk to file the same. (32)

6. And if the amount so found for such claimant shall exceed the

a greater Sum than shall have been previously offered or tendered by the said Company * * * all the Costs * * * and Expence * * * shall be defrayed by the said Company.

amount (previously offered) then judgment shall be rendered against said company for costs. (7)

7. And be it further enacted, That this act shall be deemed and taken to be a Public Act, and shall be judicially taken notice of as such by all Judges, Justices, and others, without being specially pleaded.

7. This act shall be construed favorably to effect the purposes hereby intended, and the same is hereby declared to be a public act, and copies thereof printed by authority of the State of Wisconsin shall be received as evidence thereof. (22)

Numerous other striking resemblances might be traced. Limitations on the amount of land which the company can hold, and the manner of disposing of the same, purchasing land from incapacitated persons, voting by proxy, fixing time of meeting, and the number and powers of directors, responsibility of the railroad officials to the board of directors, the power of the general meeting of stockholders over the directors, limitations on the time and amount of calls on shares, completion of the road within a specified time,— provisions on all these subjects are also much alike. The Liverpool & Manchester charter allows each share, up to twenty, one vote, and an additional vote for every four shares above twenty. This was not common to Wisconsin charters, although the same principle is involved in South Carolina charters. Among the 200 sections of the Liverpool & Manchester charter, we find a number which indicate an imperfect knowledge of railroads, due to lack of experience. Thus it contains long and minute provisions for the use of the railroad by second parties. This, as we have seen, was retained in a number of Wisconsin charters. But one of the most extraordinary provisions was that which held the operators of trains responsible for closing gates built across the railroad track: "And be it further enacted, That all Persons opening any Gate set up across the said Railway or Tramroad shall, and he, she, and they is and are hereby required, as soon as he, she, or they, and the Waggon or other Carriage under the Care of such Person or Persons, shall have passed through the same, to shut and fasten the said Gate; and every Person neglecting so to do shall forfeit and pay for every such Offence any Sum not exceeding Forty Shillings, to be levied and recovered as herein-after mentioned; and the Money arising by such Forfeiture or Forfeitures shall be applied in the manner following; that is to say, One Half Part thereof shall be paid to the Informer, and the Residue thereof to the Poor of the Township or Parish wherein such Offence shall be committed"— (sec. clxx). Curiosities of this kind could easily be multiplied. The Liverpool & Manchester charter prescribed rates and provided for their publication. It also provided for a contingencies and reserve fund. These provisions, unfortunately, slipped out of the great majority of charters granted by the Wisconsin legislature.

Wisconsin plank-road charters, also, do not essentially differ from the railroad charters. In fact, were we to take a typical plank-road or turnpike charter, and make several minor changes, such as raising the shares from $25 or $50 to $100, and substitute the word "railroad" for "plank-road," we would have a charter which in all essentials would be akin to the ordinary railroad charter.

We find, then, that Wisconsin charters do not differ much from charters of other states; and that all of them follow closely the structure of the first English charter, which in turn contained bodily many of the provisions of the English canal charters. The history of Wisconsin railroad charters thus has its origin in the English canal legislation, beginning with the middle of the eighteenth century; and canal acts, in turn, find their prototype in the turnpike acts of the seventeenth century. From the carefully-drawn, definite, and more restrictive English charters, and many of those of our Eastern states, Wisconsin charters show a gradual change towards unguarded, indefinite, and unrestrictive grants of power. The downfall of the custom of presenting memorials or petitions, or of embodying comprehensive preambles in charters, in which careful estimates of competent persons were clearly presented, and the social and economic effects of the project often prudently outlined, was no doubt a potent cause of the reckless legislation which characterized our railroad history. Surveys and estimates, on the basis of which the proper amount of capital stock might have been fixed, were usually mere guesses; although guesses even, were not always demanded. To ask for a charter was to get it, provided the proper "methods" had been employed. In case of the Liverpool & Manchester charter, the battle in parliament was fought over the preamble, which set forth the necessity of the project, and analyzed in detail its probable effects. We abandoned the preamble, and thereafter never asked whether or not the charter sought would be a benefit or a curse. We never asked whether the subscribers of stock to a half-million-dollar enterprise had ever paid even a small part of their subscription; or, whether a "prominent stockholder" in a dozen different enterprises, involving perhaps millions of "capital stock," had enough property to pay his tailor. We were westerners, with a western spirit; under the garb of push and enterprise, which pretended primarily to develop our great resources, not only the genuine railroad builder but also the "manipulator" put in his work. A spirit of carelessness on the one hand, singular credulity on the other, and a dominant combination of unscrupulous exploiters seem together to have been responsible for that heterogeneous aggregation of statutory phrases which the legislature of Wisconsin granted under the title of railroad charters. That some of the railroads built and operated under these charters have become important economic agencies can not alter these conclusions. No one would belittle the great service which our railroads have performed in the past, and which, happily, they are performing more and more effectively as time goes on. But the economic effect of a railroad is one thing; the nature of its charter as originally granted, is quite another. And in this chapter the only aim has been to present a critical and comparative view of the charters themselves.

APPENDIX.

ANALYTICAL DIGEST OF EARLY WISCONSIN RAILROAD CHARTERS, 1836-53.

The material contained in this summary was originally prepared by the author for an analytical table of charters which, because of the peculiar typographical difficulties involved, is not reproduced here. Following the same order in each charter, number 1 stands for the date of the charter; 2, for the page reference to the Laws of Wisconsin; 3, number of commissioners; 4, number of members in the board of directors; 5, capital stock; 6, size of share; 7, number of shares required to organize; 8, payment on each share required at the time of subscription; 9, maximum "calls;" 10, length of notice for calls; 11, shareholders' votes; 12, when construction of railroad must begin; 13, when the construction must be completed; 14, termini; 15, provisions for junctions, branches, and extensions; 16, to whom disputes on expropriation are referred; 17, are advantages and disadvantages considered in the valuation of land; 18, amount of land the company may hold; 19, miles of railroad which must be completed before company may open traffic; 20, provisions on rates; 21, annual report made to whom; 22, who may use railroad; 23, liability of stockholders; 24, distribution of dividends; 25, power to borrow money; 26, is power to consolidate granted; 27, other characteristics; X denotes, in the charter, an absence of provision under the head enumerated:

1. *La Fontaine R. R. Co.* 1—1836, Dec. 3; 2—1836, 33; 3—3, called "directors;" 4—X; 5—$50,000; 6—50; 7—X; 8—X; 9—X; 10—30 days; 11—X; 12—July 4, 1837; 13—5 years; 14—Winnebago City and La Fontaine; 15—X; 16—X; 17—X; 18—X; 19—X; 20—legislature may limit at any time; 21—X; 22—X; 23—X; 24—company shall divide among stockholders; 25—X; 26—X.

2. *Du Buque & Belmont.* 1—1836, Dec. 7; 2—1836, 54; 3—9; 4—7; 5—$250,000; 6—100; 7—X; 8—X; 9—X; 10—30 days; 11—X; 12—X; 13—X; 14—Belmont and some point on the Mississippi River; 15—branch to Mineral Point and Dodgeville; 16—justice of the peace notifies the sheriff, who summons a jury of eighteen persons; 17—yes; 18—sufficient for construction; holding and speculating in other lands forbidden; 19—X; 20—six cents per passenger-mile, and fifteen cents per ton-mile; 21—to stockholders, annually, by board of directors; 22—X; 23—stock liable for payment of debts, provided all debts due the company have been paid; 24—like 1, but capital stock shall remain unimpaired; 25—X; 26—X.

3. *Root River.* 1—1838, Jan. 11; 2—1837-33, 197; 3—5; 4—X; 5—$25,000; 6—50; 7—X; 8—X; 9—X; 10—30 days; 11—X; 12—July 4, 1838, and by amendment to July 4, 1839; 13—5 years; 14—at or near Ball's mill on Root River to the rapids in the same; 15—X; 16—like 2, except that jury consists of five persons; 17—X; 18—like 2; 19—X; 20—legislature may limit at any time; 21—X; 22—X; 23—X; 24—X; 25—X; 26—X; 27—there is a forfeiture clause in the time limit.

4. *Pekatonica & Mississippi.* 1—1839, March 6; 2—1838-39, 74; 3—8; 4—3; 5—$50,000; 6—100; 7—X; 8—5; 9—X; 10—30 days; 11—one vote per share; 12—3 years; 13—10 years; 14—from Mineral Point to some point on the Mississippi River in Grant county; 15—X; 16—arbritration; each party names one arbitrator; these name a third; the three together decide; may appeal to court from decision of arbitrators; 17—yes; 18—100 feet; 19—X; 20—passengers three cents per mile, freight five cents per ton-mile, and 1½ cents per ton-mile when other parties use the track; 21—legislature may demand a report at any time; 22—any person using suitable and proper carriages and paying the legal toll; 23—X; 24—everything; 25—X; 26—X; 27—if local newspapers refuse to publish notices, these shall be given by affixing the same to the door of the court house of said counties. The Territory or future State shall at any time have power to purchase said road on payment of full cost of construction and equipment, including 7 per cent. on total outlay.

5. *Michigan & Rock River.* 1—1840, Jan. 8; 2—1839-40, 12; 3—7; 4—7; 5—$100,000; 6—100; 7—X; 8—1; 9—X; 10—X; 11—one per share; 12—3 years; 13—10 years; 14—from Rock River at Illinois State line to some point on Lake Michigan in the town of Southport; 15—may build branches and junctions; 16—county commissioner, who appoints three appraisers; 17—X; 18—what may be necessary; 19—X; 20—X; 21—X; 22—X; 23—X; 24—X; 25—X; 26—yes; 27—the word "depot" is used; previously, "toll-houses" had been used, and is also found in subsequent charters; company subject to the "Act Concerning

Corporations;" this charter shall be deemed a public act and construed beneficially for all purposes herein specified or intended.

6. *Sheboygan & Fond du Lac.* 1—1847, Jan. 25; 2—1847, 23; 3–7; 4—
one president, twelve directors, and such other officers as may be
necessary; 5—$900,000; 6—100; 7—5,000; 8–5; 9—any sum; 10—30
days, and 1 per cent. per month for delayed payments; 11—one vote
per share up to five, then one vote additional for every five shares;
12—5 years; 13—15 years; 14—Sheboygan, Fond du Lac; 15—X; 16—
judge of district court to appoint 3 commissioners; 17—yes; 18—not
to exceed 80 feet in width; 19—10 miles; 20—left to company; legislature may alter or reduce tolls but not so as to bring profits of company below 12 per 'cent on investment; 21—shall report annually to
legislature; 22—X; 23—X; 24—distribute twice a year; 10 per cent of
dividends over and *above* ten per cent to be paid to the State; 25—
X; 26 –X; 27—an amendment (Feb. 11, page 180) gives company corporate power when 2,000 shares have been subscribed. It also gives
company power to transport goods by power of steam, animals, etc.,
" provided that nothing herein contained shall be construed as in
any way giving to the said company any banking privileges whatever, or any other liberties, privileges, or franchises but such as may
be necessary or incident to the making and maintaining of said railroad."

7. *Lake Michigan & Mississippi.* 1—1847, Feb. 4; 2—1847, 72; 3—26;
4—9; 5—$1,500,000; 6—100; 7—10,000; 8–5; 9—$20; 10—60 days; 11—
one per share; 12—3 years, and spend at least $50,000; 13—10 years;
14—some point on Lake Michigan south of town eight to a point on
the Mississippi River in Grant county; 15—power to connect and operate with other roads; 16—district judge appoints 3 commissioners; an
amendment of 1849 changes it to circuit judge; 17—yes; 18—4 rods
and what is necessary for construction; 19—like 6; 20—like 6; 21—
board of directors to stockholders *and* to legislature during January of each year; 22—X; 23—members of company individually liable for debts of company to amount of stock held by them; 24—X;
25—X; 26—X; 27—act to be construed like 5.

8. *Fond du Lac & Beaver Dam.* 1—1847, Feb. 10; 2—1847, 158; 3—13;
4—9; 5—$500,000; 6—50; 7—2,000; 8–5; 9—$20; 10—60 days; 11—
one vote per share; 12—10 years; 13—15 years; 14—from some eligible point in Fond du Lac county to a like point in the town of Beaver
Dam; 15—like 7; 16—like 7; 17—yes; 18—like 7; 19—like 6; 20—like
6; 21—annually to stockholders and to legislature; 22—X; 23—individually liable for debts of company to amount of stock held by
them; 24—X; 25—X; 26—X; 27—construed like 5.

9. *Milwaukee & Waukesha* (Milwaukee & Mississippi after Feb. 1,
1850). 1—1847, Feb. 11; 2—1847, 194; 3—9; 4—9; 5—$100,000; 6—

100; 7—X; 8—5; 9—$20; 10—60 days; 11—one per share; 12—3 years
and spend $20,000; 13—5 years; 14—Milwaukee, Prairieville; 15—
like 7; 16—like 7, but amended July 6, 1853, to have chief justice appoint commissioners *annually;* 17—yes; 18—like 7; 19—like 6; 20—
what company thinks reasonable; 21—annually to stockholders;
22—X; 23—like 2; 24—X; 25—X, but by amendment of Feb. 11,
1851, company empowered to borrow money " for any rate of interest
* * * any law on the subject of usury in this State or any other
State where such transactions may be made, to the contrary notwithstanding; " 26—X; 27—important amendments Feb. 1, 1850,
and Feb. 11, 1851.

10. *Madison & Beloit* (Rock River Valley Union after Feb. 9, 1851).
1—1848, Aug. 19; 2—1848, 161; 3—14; 4—9, by amendment 15; 5—
$350,000; 6 —100; 7—300; 8—5; 9—25 per cent; 10—30 days; 11—one
per share; 12—X; 13—X; 14—Beloit, Janesville, Madison; 15—
amendment of March 11, 1851, gives power to extend and connect;
16—arbitration like 4; appeal to court of proper jurisdiction; amendment like 15; 17—no; 18—100 ft.; 19—X; 20—board of directors fix;
21—X; 22—like 4; 23—X; 24—distribution of everything above 6 per
cent net on capital stock; not more than 1 per cent shall remain
undivided for more than 6 months; 25—X; 26—X; 27—shall cause
an estimate of probable costs for each mile separately to be made.
"For each mile separately," struck out by amendment of March 11,
1851.

11. *Beloit & Taycheedah.* 1—1848, Aug. 19; 2—1848, 166; 3—19; 4—12;
5—$800,000; 6—50; 7—2,000; 8—5; 9—10 per cent; 10—30 days; 11—
one per share; 12—X; 13—X; 14—Beloit (intermediate points named),
Taycheedah; 15—X; 16—like 10; 17—no; 18—100 ft.; 19—like 6; 20—
like 6; 21—to legislature; 22—like 4; 23—X; 24—like 4; 25—X; 26—
X; 27—shall cause an estimate to be made of the probable cost of
each mile separately; subject to general laws on corporations.

12. *Shullsburg Branch.* 1—1850, Feb. 9; 2—1850, 151; 3—7; 4—9; 5—
$100,000; 6—50; 7—400; 8—5; 9—25 per cent; 10—30 days; 11—one
per share; 12—X; 13—X; 14—Shullsburg to a point in the Chicago
& Galena R. R.; 15—branch north; 16—like 10; 17—no; 18—100 ft.;
19—X; 20—X; 21—like 4; 22—X; 23—like 10; 25—amendment March
11, 1851, to borrow money, and issue bonds not to exceed ¾ of the
amount actually expended; 26—X.

13. *Madison, Waterford, & Kenosha.* 1—1850, Feb. 9; 2—1850, 151;
3—7; 4—9; 5—$800,000; 6—100; 7—500; 8—5; 9—25 per cent; 10—30
days; 11—one per share; 12—X; 13—X; 14—Kenosha to any R. R. in
Rock county; 15—may extend south to State line; 16—like 4; 17—
no; 18—100 ft; 19—X; 20—X; 21—X; 22—X; 23—X; 24—X; 25—X;
26—X.

14. *Potosi & Dodgeville.* 1—1851, Feb. 10; 2—1851, 37; 3—16; 4—9; 5—
$400,000; 6—100; 7—1,000; 8—5; 9—$20; 10—60 days; 11—one per share;
12—3 years; 13—X; 14—Potosi, Dodgeville; 15—connect with any
R. R. within the limits of Grant and Iowa counties, also extend road;
16—circuit judge to appoint 3 commissioners; 17—yes; 18—5 rods;
19—like 6; 20—what company thinks reasonable; 21—to stockholders; 22—X; 23—like 2; 24—X; 25—amendment Feb. 28, 1852, power
to borrow any sum, at any rate, give bonds; 26—X; 27—forfeiture
clause; contradictory provisions on width of strip of land.

15. *Milwaukee & Fond du Lac.* 1—1851, Feb. 21; 2—1851, 72; 3—25; 4—
13; 5—$800,000; 6—100; 7—500; 8—5; 9—$10; 10—30 days; 11—one per
share; 12—3 years; 13—X; 14—Milwaukee, Iron Ridge, Fond du Lac;
15—extend termini and connect with any R. R. in Wisconsin; 16—
circuit judge appoints 3 commissioners; appeal tried by jury; 17—yes;
18—5 rods; 19—5 miles; 20—like 14; 21—X; 22—X; 23—like 2; 24—X;
25—like amendment to 9; 26—X.

16. *Madison & Swan Lake.* 1—1851, March 11; 2—1851, 172; 3—11; 4—9;
5—$500,000; 6—100; 7—300; 8—5; 9—$20; 10—60 days; 11—one per share;
12—5 years, and spend $2,000; 13—6 years; 14—defined; 15—connect
and extend; 16—like 15; 17—yes; 18—like 14; 19—like 15; 20—like 14;
21—to stockholders; 22—X; 23—X; 24—X; 25—X; 26—X.

17. *Green Bay, Milwaukee, & Chicago.* 1—1851, March 13; 2—1851, 256;
3—20; 4—9; 5—$500,000; 6—100; 7—1,000; 8—5; 9—25 per cent; 10—
30 days; 11—one per share; 12—X, but by amendment of March 4,
1852, 2 years; 13—10 years; 14—named; 15—amendment of March 4,
1852, connect and extend; 16—arbitration like 4; 17—X; 18—100 ft.;
19—X; 20—X; 21—X; 22—X; 23—X; 24—like 10; 25—like amendment
to 9; 26—X; 27—estimates required.

18. *Milwaukee & Watertown.* 1—1851, March 11; 2—1851, 180; 3—19;
4—13; 5—$500,000; 6—100; 7—500; 8—5; 9—$10; 10—30 days; 11—same
as above; 12—3 years; 13—X; 14—a specified branch; 15—extend and
connect; 16—arbitration like 4; 17—X; 18—100 ft.; 19—X; 20—X; 21—
X; 22—X; 23—X; 24—X; 25—like amendment to 9; 26—X; 27—
company not allowed to build through an orchard, garden, etc.

19. *Fort Winnebago, Baraboo Valley, & Minnesota.* 1—1851, March
13; 2—1851, 261; 3—19; 4—13; 5—$1,000,000; 6—50; 7—500; 8—5; 9—
$10; 10—30 days; 11—above; 12—3 years; 13—X; 14—northern ter-
minus not fixed; 15—connect; 16—like 15; 17—yes; 18—5 rods; 19—
like 15; 20—like 14; 21—X; 22—X; 23—like 2; 24—X; 25—like amendment to 9; 26—X.

20. *Manitowoc & Mississippi.* 1—1851, March 15; 2—1851, 373; 3—11;
4—9; 5—$1,500,000; 6—100; 7—2,000; 8—5; 9—$20; 10—60 days; 11—
above; 12—3 years and spend $50,000; 13—10 years; 14—fixed; 15—
connect; 16—like 15; 17—yes; 18—4 rods; 19—like 6; 20—like 14; 21—
to stockholders; 22—X; 23—like 2; 24—X; 25—X; 26—X.

21. *Delavan.* 1—1851, March 17; 2—1851, 414; 3—15; 4—9; [5—$200,000; 6—50; 7—4,000; 8—5; 9—25 per cent; 10—30 days; 11—above; 12—X; 13—X; 14—one fixed; 15—X; 16—arbitration like 4; 17—X; 18—100 ft.; 19—X; 20—X; 21—X; 22—X; 23—X; 24—X; 25—X; 26—X.

22. *Beloit & Madison.* 1—1852, Feb. 18; 2—1852, 55; 3—20; 4—13; 5—$1,200,000; 6—50; 7—400; 8—5; 9—X; 10—X; 11—above; 12—X; 13—X; 14—fixed route; 15—connect; 16—like 15; 17—yes; 18—100 ft.; 19—X; 20—X; 21—like 20; 22—X; 23—X; 24—distribute what exceeds 6 per cent of net profits on capital stock; 25—like amendment to 9; 26—yes.

23. *Sheboygan & Mississippi.* 1—1852, March 8; 2—1852, 154; 3—13; 4—13; 5—$3,000,000; 6—100; 7—300; 8—5; 9—$12; 10—30 days; 11—above; 12—X; 13—15 years; 14—"to Mississippi river;" 15—refusal to allow connection, carried to supreme court who appoint a commission of three; 16—any judge of supreme court appoint 3 commissioners, appeal to circuit court and have jury trial; 17—X; 18—130 ft.; 19—X; 20—X; 21—like 20; 22—X; 23—X; 24—X; 25—like amendment to 9; 26—yes.

24. *Cascade & Lake Michigan.* 1—1852, March 23; 2—1852, 235; 3—one commissioner is named, who together with stockholders shall organize; 5—$25,000; 6—X; 7—X; 8—X; 9—X; 10—X; 11—X; 12—X; 13—10; 14—entire route definitely fixed; 15—X; 16—arbitration like 4; 17—X; 18—4 rods; 19—X; 20--X; 21—X; 22—X; 23—X; 24—X; 25—X; 26—X; 27—personal and real property of company taxed like other property; labor claims first lien on property of company.

25. *Fond du Lac, Beaver Dam, Columbus,& Madison.* 1—1852, March 23; 2—1852, 254; 3—15; 4—13; 5—$1,000,000; 6—50; 7—400; 8—5; 9—$2.50; 10—30 days; 11—above; 12—3 years; 13—X; 14—named; 15—connect; 16—arbitration like 4; 17—X; 18—4 rods; 19—X; 20—X; 21—like 20; 22—X; 23—X; 24—like 22; 25—like amendment to 9; 26—X.

26. *Madison & Prairie du Chien.* 1—1852, March 24; 2—1852, 272; 3—11; 4—9; 5—$500,000; 6—100; 7—1,000; 8—5; 9—$20; 10—60 days; 11—above; 12—5 years; 13—X; 14—named; 15—connect; 16—like 15; 17—yes; 18—5 rods; 19—like 6; 20—like 14; 21—like 20; 22—X; 23—like 2; 24—X; 25—X; 26—X; 27—special grant of power to connect.

27. *Green Bay & Lake Superior.* 1—1852, March 24; 2—1852, 283; 3—9; 4—9; 5—$500,000; 6—50; 7--1,000; 8—5; 9--10 per cent; 10—30 days; 11—above; 12—X; 13—X; 14—general; 15—X; 16—like 15; 17—X; 18—100 ft.; 19—like 6; 20—like 6; 21—to stockholders and legislature; 22—like 4; 23—X; 24—like 4; 25—X; 26—X; 27—estimate required.

28. *La Crosse & Milwaukee.* 1--1852, April 2; 2—1852, 325; 3—17; 4—7; 5—$4,000,000; 6—100; 7—500; 8—5; 9 and 10—left to directors; 11--above; 12—3; 13—10; 14—named; 15—connect and build branches; the latter repealed on April 19, 1852; 16—judge of county court

or chairman of county board of supervisors appoint three arbitrators; 17—X; 18—100 ft.; 19—like 15; 20—X; 21—like 20; 22—X;
23—like 2, repealed April 19, 1852; 24—X; 25—like amendment to 9;
26—power to purchase or lease other roads; special provision for a
probable congressional land grant.

29. *Southern Wisconsin.* 1—1852, April 10; 2—1852, 363; 3—9; 4—9 to
15; 5—$1,500,000; 6—100; 7—700; 8—X; 9—$12; 10—30 days; 11—
above; 12—2; 13—X; 14—"to some point on Mississippi;" 15—connect; 16—like 23; 17—yes; 18—130 ft.; 19—X; 20—X; 21—like 20;
22—X; 23—X; 24—X; 25—like amendment to 9; 26—yes.

30. *Madison, Ft. Atkinson, & Whitewater.* 1—1852, April 14; 2—1852,
487; 3—18; 4—13; 5—$800,000; 6—50; 7—200; 8—5; 9—$2.50; 10—30
days; 11—above; 12—3 years; 13—X; 14—named; 15—connect and
"operate with other railroads;" 16—like 15; 17—X; 18—100 ft.;
19—X; 20—X; 21—like 20; 22—X; 23—X; 24—like 22; 25—like amendment to 9; 26—"to operate other railroads."

31. *Portage City, Stevens Point, & Wausau.* 1—1852, April 16; 2—
1852, 553; 3—13; 4—9; 5—$1,000,000; 6—X; 7—100,000; 8—5; 9—25
per cent; 10—30 days; 11—above; 12—X; 13—X; 14—named; 15—X;
16—arbitration like 4; 17—X; 18—100 ft.; 19—X; 20—X; 21—X;
22—X; 23—X; 24—X; 25—like amendment to 9; 26—X.

32. *Racine, Janesville, & Mississippi.* 1—1852, April 17; 2—1852, 591;
3—13; 4—13; 5—$3,000,000; 6—100; 7—300; 8—5; 9—$12; 10—30 days;
11—above; 12—5 years; 13—10 years; 14—named; 15—connect; 16—
like 23; 17—yes; 18—130 ft.; 19—X; 20—X; 21—like 20; 22—X;
23—X; 24—X; 25—like amendment to 9; 26—yes; amendment of
March 19, 1853, authorizes company to build by sections.

33. *Mineral Point.* 1—1852, April 17; 2—1852, 624; 3—16; 4—9, amended
to 5 to 15; 5—$500,000; 6—100; 7—1,000; 8—5; 9—$20; 10—60 days;
11—above; 12—3 years; 13—X; 14—general; 15—connect and operate
with other railroads; 16—like 15; 17—X; 18—5 rods; 19—like 6;
20—like 14; 21—like 20; 22—X; 23—like 2; 24—X; 25—like amendment to 9; 26—X; 27—may increase stock.

34. *Northwestern.* 1—1852, April 17; 2—1852, 646; 3—5; 4—9 to 13;
5—$2,000,000; 6—100; 7—500; 8—X; 9—$12; 10—30 days; 11—
above; 12—10 years; 13—X; 14—general; 15—connect; 16—like
23; 17—yes; 18—130 ft.; 19—X; 20—X; 21—like 20; 22—reciprocal use of railroads, cars, engines, etc., each to use the R. R. of
other; in case of disagreement as to terms, the supreme court appoints a commission who shall fix the terms of such reciprocal use;
23—X; 24—X; 25—like amendment to 9 (?); 26—yes.

35. *Milwaukee & Horicon.* 1—1852, April 17; 2—1852, 675; 3—9; 4—7;
5—$800,000; 6—100; 7—500; 8—5; 9—$10; 10—30 days; 11—above;
12—5 years; 13—15 years; 14—named; 15—connect and operate with
others; extension specifically provided for; 16—like 15; 17—yes; 18—

5 rods; 19—like 15; 20—like 14; 21—like 20; 22—X; 23—like 2; 24—X;
25—like amendment to 9; 26—implied (?).

36. *Watertown & Berlin.* 1—1853, Feb. 11; 2—1853, 21; 3—41; 4—
fifteen to be chosen at first election, 7 to 20; 5—$1,000,000; 6—100;
7—100; 8—5 per cent; 9 and 10—left to board of directors; 11—
above; 12—3 years; 13—10 years; 14—general; 15—connect and
operate; 16—arbitration, special; 17—X; 18—100 ft.; 19—like 15;
20—like 14; 21—like 20; 22—X; 23—X; 24—X; 25—at any rate,
"any law on the subject of usury in this State notwithstanding;"
26—X, may lease or purchase.

37. *Michigan & Wisconsin Transit.* 1—1853, Feb. 28; 2—1853, 60;
3—eighteen who at once form a body corporate; these elect nine
directors; 5—$6,000,000 to $15,000,000; 6—100; 7—2,000; 8—5 per
cent; 9—left to board of directors; never to exceed $100 per share;
10—30 days; 11—above; 12—X; 13—15 years; 14—general; 15—connect; 16—arbitration, special; 17—X; 18—100 ft.; 19—X; 20—like
14; 21—to stockholders and legislature; 22—any person who gets
license from company; 23—like personal property; 24—annual or
semi-annual distribution; 25—any amount; 26—may connect themselves in business; 27—provisions on discrimination; banking, brokerage, and dealing in produce is prohibited; taxes, first lien; carry
U. S. mail; elaborate report required.

38. *Kenosha & Beloit.* 1—1853, March 4; 2—1853, 121; 3—14; 4—13,
and 7 to 15; 5—$100,000; 6—100; 7—400; 8—5; 9 and 10—left to
directors; 11—above; 12—3 years and spend $25,000; 13—X; 14—
named; 15—connect, purchase, lease; 16—like 36; 17—X; 18—100
ft.; 19—like 15; 20—like 14; 21—like 20; 22—X; 23—X; 24—X;
25—any sum, any rate; 26—yes; 27—by-laws not to be inconsistent
with constitution of U. S. or of State.

39. *Wisconsin Central.* 1—1853, March 4; 2—1853, 131; 3—23; 4—
like 38; 5—$1,000,000; 6—100; 7—200; 8—5; 9 and 10—left to direct-
ors; 11—above; 12—3; 13—10; 14—general; 15—connect, operate,
lease, or purchase; 16—supreme or circuit judge appoints 3 commissioners; 17—X; 18—100 ft.; 19—like 15; 20—like 14; 21—like 20;
22—X; 23—X; 24—X; 25—like 38; 26—yes.

40. *Green Bay & Minnesota.* 1—1853, March 7; 2—1853, 147; 3—16;
4—13, and 5 to 15; 5—$4,000,000; 6—100; 7—1,000; 8—5; 9 and 10—
like 39; 11—above; 12—3, and spend $25,000 in 10 years; 13—X;
14—general; 15—connect, operate, lease, purchase; 16—like 36; 17—
X; 18—100 ft.; 19—like 15; 20—like 14; 21—like 20; 22—X; 23—
like 2; 24—X; 25—like 36; 26—implied; 27—100 feet through State
lands granted.

Other charters were analyzed, but this summary of the
first forty is probably sufficient to illustrate the author's
methods, and data upon which the second chapter is based.